SURA'S

- Biography Series -

SAINTS OF THE MASSES

By
Suman Bhat

FIRST EDITION
An imprint of Sura Books (Pvt) Ltd.
(An ISO 9001:2000 Certified Company)
Chennai ● Ernakulam ● Bengalooru

Price: Rs.50.00

© PUBLISHERS

SAINTS OF THE MASSES

BY
Suman Bhat

This Edition : August, 2008

Size : 1/8 Demy

Pages : 96

Price: Rs.50.00
ISBN: 81-7478-630-9

FIRST EDITION
[An imprint of Sura Books (Pvt) Ltd.]

Head Office: 1620, 'J' Block, 16th Main Road, Anna Nagar, **Chennai - 600 040.**
Phones: 044-26162173, 26161099.

Branches : ● XXXII/2328, New Kalavath Road, Opp. to BSNL, Near Chennoth Glass, Palarivattom, **Ernakulam - 682 025.** Phones: 0484-3205797, 2535636

● 3638/A, IVth Cross, Opp. to Malleswaram Railway Station, Gayathri Nagar, Back gate of Subramaniya Nagar, **Bengalooru - 560 021.** Phone: 080-23324950

Printed at T. Krishna Press, Chennai - 600 102 and Published by V.V.K.Subburaj for First Edition [An imprint of Sura Books (Pvt) Ltd.] 1620, 'J' Block, 16th Main Road, Anna Nagar, Chennai - 600 040. Phones: 26162173, 26161099. Fax: (91) 44-26162173. e-mail: enquiry@surabooks.com; website: www.surabooks.com

08 08 1000

DEDICATION

With grateful thanks, this humble effort is
dedicated at the lotus feet of Lord Sri Krishna

ACKNOWLEDGEMENTS

I thank Dr. Smt.Veena Raj, for her kindness in lending
me reference material for Amma's biography. I thank my
husband Raghu and children Akshay and Niyathi, my parents
Smt. & Sri. S.R.S. Murthy, my in- laws, Smt. & Sri. N.V. Bhat,
Mamtha-Ravish, Prathima-Sudhindra, Lekha-Kishore and
their families for their love, support and words of
encouragement.

Matha Amritanandamayi- "The Hugging Saint"

Contents

BIOGRAPHY SERIES

SAINTS OF THE MASSES

MATHA AMRITANANDAMAYI

Amma or **Matha Amritanandamayi**, the world famous saint is more popularly known as the "Hugging Saint." The name is indicative of her nature which is the  nectarean flow of love and affection that she transfers to every living entity. 'Amrita' means 'nectar' and Matha Amritanandamayi means the Mother who is the abode of the nectar of love and 'Ananda' - bliss that she distributes unconditionally to everyone who comes into contact with her. She is, therefore, also known as the 'Mother of Immortal Bliss'.

The world seems to have become a smaller place, as waves of Amma's love and compassion are flooding it unceasingly in ever-increasing concentric circles, touching all parts of the earth. She preaches and practises pure love, dharma and truth as the religion, which will unite the whole world.

The lives of many saints have been a saga of trials and tribulations. Anyone who reads about the life-stories of most of these saints are left wondering why these saints who provide solace and comfort to thousands of people who flock to them have had to undergo immense suffering themselves. Probably it is God's way of showing how his Grace starts working in the lives of those people who hold on steadfastly to his feet despite obstacles and hardships. It also serves as an example to those people who lose heart easily when they have to face troubled times and suffering. They derive strength from reading about these saints and face life with renewed confidence and courage.

Amma's life-story is a similar revelation and eye-opener. It is the story of a simple girl from a fisherman's family, who without any formal education or training and in the face of tremendous opposition and hardships has today become a much loved and honoured saint. She has been providing solace and love to millions of suffering people all over the world. All through the period when she had to undergo immense suffering and upheavals, there was one constant factor that always steered her clear of all the troubles she had to face - and that was the intense love and yearning and devotion she had and has towards the Lord. She never let go of the Lord's feet and the Lord never let her down.

Background and legends associated with the sacred place of Amma's birth:

There is a small village called Parayakadavu which formed a part of the Alappad Panchayat (a group of five villages) in Kollam District, Kerala State. A family called Idamannel owned a small part of the land in Parayakadavu. The hereditary work of this family was fishing; the family observed many religious customs. Many people born in this family had become ardent devotees of the Lord. Shri Velayudhan and his wife Shrimathi Madhavi were a couple belonging to this family. They were very pious by nature and generous towards others. Velayudhan would always distribute a few fish from the day's catch, free of cost to the poor villagers. A handful of coins from the day's sales would first be distributed to a few children. Their first son was named Sugunanandan - He became a very sincere devotee of Lord Krishna, who was worshipped daily in their homes. As a small boy, Sugunanandan learnt Kathakali (a classical dance-drama form of Kerala), which depicts the pastimes of Gods and Goddesses. Sugunanandan always loved to portray Sri Krishna. He would become so overwhelmed by emotion while doing this that he would sometimes fall unconscious on the stage.

The Idamannel compound was skirted by backwaters on three sides. There was a lush growth of vegetation, and coconuts, fruits and cashew trees grew in plenty. Once Sugunanandan (as a young boy of 13 or 14 years of age) was climbing the cashew trees with his cousin and enjoying the delicious cashew fruit when he saw a Sannyasi with long hair and beard, walking towards Idamannel. To their surprise, the Sannyasi laughed and proclaimed loudly, "I can see many ascetics immersed in deep meditation in this place. Previously, this was the abode of many great souls whose tombs lie under this land. Many Sannyasis will attain liberation here. This will become a holy place." He then continued on his way. Sugunanandan and his cousin were deeply puzzled; many years later, they wonderingly recalled the prophetic words of this Sannyasi. This was when Sudhamani, the little daughter of Sugunanandan later grew into a holy saint of such stature that she attracted millions of disciples who came from all over the world to the ashram she built there.

There is a wonderful legend associated with Parayakadavu village. The people of this village were a small clan of fishermen who could trace their ancestry as far back as Sage Parasara. It was Sage Parasara who married Satyavati; she became the mother of Shri Veda Vyasa, the famous sage who codified the Vedas, and the author of the divine scriptures, the Mahabharata and Shrimad Bhagavata. There are other legends which talk about the sanctity and greatness of this village. Once, Lord

Subramanya, son of Lord Shiva and Goddess Parvati incurred the displeasure of his father for having committed a great mistake and Lord Shiva cursed him and so he had to take birth in the body of a fish. When Mother Parvati tried to intervene, Lord Shiva cursed her also and she had to take birth in a fisherman's clan, as daughter of their King. All this was but a Lila (divine play) of the Lord. Lord Shiva told them that he would liberate them at an appropriate time.

In the sea of Alappad, Lord Subramanya, as a whale, created terror and tore the nets of the fishermen and overturned their boats; despite many efforts, nobody could capture the whale. They could not pursue their livelihood for fear of the whale. The King of the fishermen announced that he would give his daughter (Goddess Parvati reborn, but none of them knew this then) in marriage to any man who captured the whale. An old man came to Alappad one day and with the permission of the King, threw a rope into the sea. To everyone's amazement, the whale which had eluded capture for so long, was bound by the rope; the old man asked the fishermen to drag the whale to the shore while chanting a particular mantra. When the whale was finally dragged to the shore it suddenly took the form of Lord Subramanya who blessed everyone and disappeared. The old man demanded that the daughter of the king be wed to him as per the King's promise. The King was wondering how to give away his young daughter in marriage to such an old man, when the princess herself came forward and told her father that truth was their religion and anyone who forsook truth would have to face hell. She said that she was ready to marry the old man and follow him. When the old man was asked which his hometown (uru) was, he replied enigmatically that he had no particular dwelling place. Any place he stopped would become his uru, that is, his hometown. Accordingly, the place where they stopped came to be called 'Chellunna Uru' (meaning, the place reached). This is the modern day Chenganoor in Alappad. At Chellunna uru, the old man and the princess suddenly transformed into the images of Lord Shiva and Goddess Parvati in front of the wonderstruck villagers, who realized that they had also been a part of this divine drama! To this day, the villagers of Alappad go to the village of Chenganoor to perform the marriage rites of Lord Shiva and Goddess Parvati. One year, when the villagers feeling disinclined to go all the way to Chenganoor, did not go there to perform the annual ritual, strange events occurred in the Chenganoor temple. The decorated elephant that was to carry the image of the Lord refused to move even an inch forward. At Alappad, small pox broke out and the repentant villagers immediately went in a procession to Chenganoor to perform the auspicious ritual there. From then on, nobody dared to do away with the custom.

It is the same coastal landscape associated with such sacred lore that was soon to become the centreplace for another divine drama.

Birth and childhood:

Sugunanandan was married to Damayanti, a very pious lady. They had 13 children of whom eight survived. The third amongst those eight children was named Sudhamani, which meant 'Ambrosial or Nectarean Jewel'. The name they gave her proved to be significant, as years later, she came to be known as Mother Amritanandamayi, the mother who distributed the nectar (Amrita also means nectar) of love and compassion to millions of people.

Damayanti had strange visions and dreams when she was expecting her fourth child. She had wonderful dreams wherein a saintly figure handed her a golden idol of Sri Krishna. Another night she beheld Lord Shiva and Devi, the Divine Mother. At around the same time, Sugunanandan too began having dreams of the Divine Mother. They felt that some good fortune would be theirs, because of all these auspicious signs.

One night, Damayanti dreamt that she had given birth to Sri Krishna and she was feeding him her milk. The next day, as she was working by the seashore, she felt a sudden urge to go to her hut for she felt that she was about to deliver. She went to the hut, planning to take a few things with her to her mother's house but before she could do anything, she delivered the baby without any pain or discomfort. There was nobody to help her out at that time; the atmosphere by the seaside was peaceful and silent. She noticed that the baby was a girl. She was worried that the baby did not cry but was astonished to see a beaming smile on the child's face - The child's eyes were open and looked penetratingly at Damayanti. The gaze touched her heart and years later, she would recall that look and say that she had never been able to forget that deep gaze of the child. A lady passing by at that moment saw what had happened and quickly made the mother and child comfortable and ran to inform the others. So, on 27th September 1953, unknown to others, a Mahatma (a great soul) had quietly appeared in the world in a small hut by the shore of the deep blue Arabian Sea.

The parents were very puzzled about three things soon after her birth - one was the child's dark blue complexion; another was that the baby lay in padmasana (the lotus posture of sitting during Hatha Yoga); and thirdly, she was holding her fingers in chinmudra with the tips of her thumb and forefinger touching to form a circle. The parents were worried for they attributed this dark blue complexion to some strange disease and the position she lay in to some abnormality in bone structure. The doctors put a rest to their fears telling them that the child was completely normal. In their anxiety, they seemed to have forgotten their lovely dreams and the fact that the complexion of their baby was the dark blue colour associated both with Lord Sri Krishna and Divine Mother Kali. The baby was named Sudhamani.

As the child grew up, the blue colour turned into dark brown, but would re-appear years later when Mother started exhibiting Krishna Bhava and Devi Bhava. Many unusual signs that were understood only years later marked her development in the early years. Small babies usually turn over on their bellies initially, and slowly begin to crawl and after some months get up holding onto a chair or a table and then slowly learn to walk with faltering steps. In Sudhamani's case, none of stages occurred. She was a baby of six months, when, one day, to everyone's surprise she just got up and walked without faltering. Soon after, she began running also, to the delight of her family. She started speaking Malayalam, her mother tongue, as early as when she was just six months of age. When she was two years, she, without instructions from anyone, began to exhibit a passion for chanting the divine names of Lord Sri Krishna. Her habit of chanting the divine names of the Lord continues to this day. At that tender age, she began to sing short prayers and songs in praise of Sri Krishna! By the time she was four, she had begun to compose one or two line songs on Sri Krishna and sang them with devotion. She exhibited wonderful virtuous qualities like love for God, affection for others, concern for the poor and needy even when she was that tiny. The villagers felt a strange fascination for these endearing qualities and called her 'Kunju', which means 'little one'.

At the age of five, she was composing lovely and poignant devotional songs in praise of Lord Sri Krishna. She would call upon the Lord as the blue-hued Divine power in golden yellow silk garments who played the flute, who had destroyed Putana and many demons and who was the Govardhana Giridhari who protected the residents of Gokula from torrential rains - She would beseech him to hear her prayers and give her his darshan and help all the poor residents of the village. When she was not singing, she would be found meditating in solitude in some lonely corner. Because her behaviour was so unusual and very different from those of ordinary children, her parents, not understanding the divinity manifest in her, would often scold her and tell her to play some games with the other children. But even then, the only games she liked to play were enacting the pastimes of Lord Sri Krishna. She would call other children 'Krishna' and pray to them and offer them fruits and milk as 'naivedyam' (offering to the Lord). Sometimes, the children would get scared, but most of the time, they loved to be with Sudhamani because she sang divinely and was loving and affectionate to all. She could, with very little effort, make all the children sing songs in praise of Lord Krishna. At the age of seven, one of the songs she wrote in Malayalam was:

> Protect me, O Supreme Lord who resides
>
> In the city of Guruvayoor,
>
> O Child Krishna, who acted as a cowherd boy,
>
> O Lord of the Universe, Consort of Goddess Lakshmi,
>
> Protect me, O Lord Krishna, Beloved of Radha,
>
> O Krishna, the Beloved of Gopis.
>
> O Krishna, the son of Nanda,
>
> O Krishna, who is worshipped and adored by everyone.

Her parents were stunned to see her dance in God-intoxicated bliss. Nobody had taught her how to dance; but at that age, without receiving any kind of spiritual instruction, she would lose herself in singing devotional songs. In her family, nobody could understand her divine moods. They put it down to her being an eccentric and over-imaginative child. A song composed by her at the age eight shows her intense yearning to attain darshan of her Lord:

> O Essence of Mercy, O Compassionate One,
>
> O Krishna, give me refuge!
>
> O Krishna, is the story of the burning tears
>
> That flow unknown to thee?
>
> Offering flowers at thy feet that have
>
> Crushed the serpent Kaaliya.
>
> I will worship thee, O Krishna;
>
> Thou didst come as the charioteer of Arjuna
>
> At Kurukshetra to protect Truth and Righteousness

O Lord who preserves Dharma, Show a bit of compassion
to us!

O Lord of the Gita, lover of divine music,

Give the capacity to sing thy songs

O lover of devotional singing,

Do you not hear thy sacred names

Uttered from my innermost heart?

A constant stream of tears would run down her face as she
wept for her beloved Krishna; the villagers marvelled at the
intensity of devotion in a child so young! They still had no idea
what a great soul she was. At school, Sudhamani proved to be a
brilliant student with an astonishing memory. She topped in all
the subjects and could recite any lesson or poem just by hearing
it said once, like a 'Srutidhara' (one who can recite from memory
any passage, however long, just by hearing it once). The teachers
simply loved her.

By the time she was nine, she was in the fourth grade. This
little girl had a very difficult time at home, as she was made to
perform most of the household chores. Her elder sister Kasturi
was attending a local college and elder brother Subhagan was
in school. Damayanti did not want their studies disturbed and
was very tough with Sudhamani, whose dark colour and strange
behaviour also contributed towards causing untold hardship to
her. The mother looked down on her with disdain and expected
that she be the unpaid servant of the household. It is difficult to
even imagine how a mother could be so cruel towards her tender
young daughter, but Sudhamani bore all this with tremendous
patience. Damayanti had borne five more children after
Sudhamani and her health had deteriorated completely. Apart
from this, financial problems were another burden in a house
with so many children. It seemed as if she would vent all her
frustrations on poor Sudhamani. Sudhamani had become
Damayanti's punching bag. Our hearts go out to the little child
who had to bear so much cruelty, but one realized later that

God has a reason for everything. In Sudhamani's case, it served to make her detached and aloof from worldly affairs at a very early age.

Sudhamani had to sweep and clean the house and compound, tend to the cows and milk them, had to fetch water for cooking and also had to scrub vessels and wash the family's clothes. She also had to help in getting the younger children dressed and ready for school. All this was such a burden on the little child, that at age ten, she had to discontinue her studies and concentrate on the work at home. Sudhamani felt sad but did not complain to anyone. Any time she had after attending to all the chores, she would spend in meditating and then singing to the Lord. In a small room built next to the cowshed alongside the main house, she would sit looking at the picture of her deity Sri Krishna, which she always kept with her. She would pour out her heart and sorrow only to him.

The child had an exceptionally kind heart. Her heart melted when she saw the sufferings of the villagers. She would steal milk, curds and butter from the house and help a few of the starving families nearby. She would take the money from her mother's collection box and use it to buy foodstuff for the poor people of the village. Or she would take dry food items from her own family's meager store and give it to the needy. Damayanti beat her mercilessly whenever she was caught, but Sudhamani bore it patiently. Despite the fact that she did most of the household chores without help from anyone, Damayanti's list of complaints against her would not end. She complained so much to Sugunanandan that even Sudhamani, the epitome of patience burst out in sorrow one day at the amount of torment she had to face, saying, "I am not your daughter, I must be your daughter-in-law. That is why you hate me so much!"

Almost everyone looked upon girls who had discontinued their studies as potential unpaid servants. Families would ask for their services in performing kitchen and household chores. Sudhamani, at the age of 13 had to go to her grandmother's house 6 km south of Parayakadavu. She could reach there either by travelling on a boat on the backwaters or walking 6 km along the shores of the Arabian Sea. She went a few times by boat, but her mother put a stop to that by saying it was a waste of money and told her to walk instead! Sudhamani did not mind the lovely long walk on the beach; she called the ocean her mother and the blue waves constantly reminded her of Krishna. She often ran towards the waves as if to embrace them. One is reminded of Sri Chaitanya Mahaprabhu, a great saint who often jumped into the waters of the River Yamuna and the Sea whenever he was in their proximity, saying that he saw Krishna in them. His followers had to literally drag him back to the shore. Similarly, many a time, the villagers had to pull Sudhamani back from the waves! To her, the sound of the ocean waves seemed like 'Aum', the divine primordial sound! She felt that Krishna was touching her when she felt the breeze from the ocean. She would suddenly lose external consciousness and sit meditating on the sand, unaware of anything else. She would have preferred to stay there for hours, but she had work to do at her grandmother's house. Somehow she would manage to pull herself out of the exalted states she kept lapsing into and continue on her way to her grandmother's house. At her grandmother's and various uncles and aunts' houses she had to go, she had to toil endlessly, performing various tasks; she even had to ferry her cousins along the backwaters to and fro from school. This was one task that she really enjoyed, as she could lose herself in singing about Krishna then. She had to boil unhusked rice paddy and dry it in the sun. She had to wash everyone's clothes, cook and clean and scrub the vessels. Carrying pots of hot rice gruel on her head had caused the hair to fall off from a part of her tender head. Her cousins, instead of trying to help or appreciate her for all the hard work she had to do for them, taunted her and teased her endlessly because of her devotion to Krishna and her habit of constantly singing songs in praise of him. She had to fetch drinking water in a boat from a place quite a distance away. On these boat-rides, rowing along the beautiful backwaters, she would delight in the natural scenery. She would question the ripples in the backwaters saying - "O little waves! Have you seen Krishna who is of the colour of a dark blue storm cloud? Can you hear the enchanting music of his flute?" She would look up at the swiftly moving clouds in the sky and address them thus - "O dark blue clouds! Where have you hidden my Krishna? O Cranes flying in the sky, are you going to Vrindavan? If you meet Krishna, tell him of this little child who is always weeping and waiting for his darshan." One is reminded of the Gopi's moods in Vrindavan, when Krishna had gone away to Mathura. They would roam around the forests asking every creeper and plant and bird and animal about their dear Krishna. They had named the various ingredients they kept in their jars in the kitchen with various names of the Lord like Hari, Vaasudeva, Govinda, Gopala etc. While selling the milk and curds in the streets of Vrindavana, they did not call out saying milk, butter or curds - they said Krishna or Nanda Kumara or Yashoda-nandana! While performing their daily tasks, their thoughts would be immersed in Krishna and Krishna alone. Theirs was a sacred, deep and unselfish love, fully submerged in thought of Krishna. Sudhamani's case was not different. Every task she performed, she had the Lord's name on her lips. Even when somebody scolded or beat her, it had no effect, because her thoughts were always immersed in the Lord. Her thoughts, mind and deeds were all dedicated to her Lord Sri Krishna.

Meanwhile, the habit of pilfering foodstuff from the house to help the poor and needy got her into a lot of trouble with her uncle and aunt. She was severely beaten several times but it only made her more and more philosophical. At that age, she understood the impermanent nature of the world. She realized that the world was full of sorrow and every relationship was need-based. There was no selfless love that she could see anywhere. She turned fully towards God as she felt that only God loved everyone with a selfless love. Only His love was unconditional and eternally compassionate.

Things reached a stage when Sudhamani realized that she had to get out of the clutches of her relatives if she had to pursue her spiritual practices. She created a circumstance that led to a big fight with her uncle and aunt. She also argued heatedly for once. The relatives, unable to accept that a quiet person like her could also rebel, callously took back all the money and gifts they had given her for working for them and sent her home empty-handed. A pained Sudhamani had then exclaimed; "One day, you'll have to come to me for help. Until then, I will never enter this house." God always understands the pain his devotees go through. Eleven years later, that particular family had to face a severe financial crisis and other hardships. Sudhamani had become a famous saint by then and they went to request her to come to their house and bestow her blessings on all of them! Sudhamani's aunt repented and apologized for her cruel behaviour saying – "Oh! How could I have scolded and beaten the little one. I never imagined she would become such a great saint." Many incidents like this only go to prove that God does care for his devotees and he frees them from their tormentor's clutches. His ways may be strange, but when least expected, he heals the pain of his devotees and wipes away their tears.

After Sudhamani returned to her mother's house from her uncle's house, she had to face more torture from her family, especially from her mother Damayanti and brother Subhagan. She began to spend more time in devotional singing and prayers and meditation. If she heard any rendering of the Srimad Bhagavatam, she would lose touch with external consciousness and be transported into a state of bliss. She had visions of a dark-blue and sometimes reddish-complexioned Krishna playing on the flute, Krishna talking to her and holding her hand and showing her the glory of so many different worlds. She would hear the sound of the flute nearby, but later realize that the enchanting music was coming from within her own heart. Whenever she came back to awareness of the external world, she had a backbreaking workload to attend to. Her compassion towards the poor and needy was increasing and she took her

2

mother's gold bangle, sold it, and used it to feed the poor. Her mother beat her mercilessly. She even used a pestle and a machete once to strike her on an occasion when Sudhamani had retorted back after a scolding. She was not allowed to wear good clothes. When she tried applying vermilion on her forehead, her brother forbade her from doing so. When she tried to wear colourful clothes like her sisters, Damayanti and Subhagan taunted her cruelly because of her colour; they treated her like a menial servant and expected her to dress like one. Sudhamani somehow managed to stitch her own clothes using the old and discarded clothes of her sisters and brother. Why this child amongst all the other children was treated so shabbily is beyond the scope of human conjecture. She slogged endlessly for everyone in the family, but was destined to hear only heaps of verbal abuse from them during those years. After many years, Sudhamani would say, "All those endless ordeals, trials and tribulations only proved to me the ephemeral nature of human relationships. They showed me the right path, the path towards God-realization. It showed her that God was the only goal to be pursued. God was the only one who could give unconditional love and protection."

Subhagan would scream at her when she sang her prayers. He and his mother and some others in the family were convinced that her excessive display of devotion was a form of madness. How could they understand the ecstatic states of a Mahatma - a God-realized soul? So, their cruelty and taunts towards her continued. Her parents would take all the children on functions and visits, but leave Sudhamani behind. At times such as those, Sudhamani would pour her heart out to Krishna in the puja room. Her tears were for Krishna alone. When she had her visions of Krishna, she would identify with Radha so completely that she would dance ecstatically and gracefully and it would stun anyone who happened to watch her. It was around this time, that, unknown to others, she had identified so completely with Krishna that she often felt she was Krishna herself. Once her state of inner absorption in the Supreme was so intense that she had no wish to return to external awareness. It was then that she heard a voice within her saying, "Thousands and thousands of people in the world are steeped in misery. I have much for you to do, you who are one with me." It was brought home to her then that Krishna had sent her into the material world to do his work. She suddenly realized that she knew everything about anyone she saw. She experienced no particular feelings of greatness at those initial manifestations of Krishna Bhava. She only felt intense compassion for the suffering people and came to know of their suffering and problems even before being told.

It was at this stage that she suddenly started manifesting Krishna Bhava, the mood of Krishna. She was passing by a house when she heard some verses from Srimad Bhagavatam being rendered. She went into the house and stood in front of the astonished devotees; her inner identification with Krishna transformed her features and movements into those of Sri Krishna and the people felt as if Lord Krishna had appeared in their midst. She sprinkled holy water on all the devotees gathered there. A few skeptics wanted her to show some miracle to prove that she really had the power of Krishna within her. Initially, she refused saying that there was divinity existing within everyone and there was no need for a miracle to show that divinity had manifested in all its glory within her. But when people still insisted, at the next Bhagavatam reading held at the same house, she asked the devotees to bring a vessel of water. Having sanctified it with Tulasi leaves, she sprinkled the holy water on everyone and then asked one of the devotees to dip his hand into the holy water. To his and everyone's amazement, the water turned into milk. Another devotee was asked to dip his hands into the milk. This time, the milk turned into 'panchamritam' (a mixture of milk, bananas, curds, raisins, rock sugar offered often as naivedyam-offerings to the Lord). This was distributed as prasad to the people gathered there. There were more than a thousand people gathered there including the skeptics who were waiting to expose her as a fraud. They declared that everyone had been hypnotized and the panchamritam would vanish soon. But it did not; the vessel remained full to the brim even after its contents had been distributed to everyone gathered there. Its fragrance remained on people's hands for days afterwards. Many people became convinced that some form of divine power existed in Sudhamani. From then on, Sudhamani regularly manifested Krishna Bhava near a Banyan tree on the Idamannel property. A few believed in her divine power and came for Darshan; the non-believers came hoping to prove that she was a fraud. Some came out of curiosity. Many people experienced relief from their sufferings and got solutions to their problems and word of this spread. People from all over Kerala and later from all over India started coming for darshan on Krishna Bhava days. One is reminded of Sri Chaitanya Mahaprabhu (a great saint who is believed to be an incarnation of Radha and Krishna) when he gave a Maha Bhava Darshan, which came to be known as 'Maha Prakash' or 'Shat Prahariya Bhava', when he appeared to each of his devotees in the form they held most dear. He told them of their past lives and revealed to them how he had helped them when they had been facing various problems. He appeared as Sri Ram to one Murari Gupta, a devotee of Lord Sri Ram and had accepted worship from Shrivasa Thakura, another devotee of his, telling him that he was the Lord Narasimha who Shrivasa had been worshipping. He had given him darshan in the same form.

Lord Chaitanya Mahaprabhu was seen predominantly exhibiting two Bhavas - one in which he was mostly seen was that of a devotee (God in the form of a devotee); the other was the 'Bhagavat Bhava', where he manifested the power latent within him and revealed his real state of self-abidance. He would reveal himself in the forms that were most favorite to them, forms of Sri Rama, Sri Krishna, Sri Narasimha and others. Ma Anandamayee of Bengal would exhibit Krishna Bhava and Kali Bhava while singing Bhajans. Sri Ramakrishna Paramahansa would exhibit more than one Bhava too. It is said that during his period of Hanuman Sadhana, he had even developed a small tail like Hanuman. Likewise Mata Amritanandamayi exhibits the

Bhavas in which the most devotees like to see her. In the holy scriptures, it is said that the incarnations of God fall into three main categories: (1) Purnavataras (full or perfect), (2) Amsa Avataras (partial manifestation) and (3) Avesha Avataras (temporary overshadowing by divine power).

Sri Krishna is believed to be a Purnavatara-the Supreme power, the Supreme energy assuming a human form and manifesting infinite power without any limitation. He comes to preserve righteousness and destroy the evil prevalent in society. Sri Krishna says in the Bhagavad Gita:

"Paritranaaya Saadhunam, Vinashayacha Duskritam,

Dharma samsthapanarthaya, Sambhavami Yuge Yuge"

This means, "to deliver the pious and to annihilate the miscreants, I myself appear millennium after millennium.

Once, when Lord Sri Krishna was residing in Dwaraka, he expressed a desire to see his dear devotee, Sri Hanuman. He sent his Vahana, Sri Garuda, the King of birds to fetch Hanuman who was meditating in the Kadali Vanam. Hanuman refused to see Sri Krishna saying he would see no one except his beloved Sri Rama. When Garuda Deva conveyed this message to Sri Krishna, the Lord smiled and sent him back with another message that Lord Rama and Mother Sita had come to Dwaraka and they wanted to see Hanuman. By the time Hanuman reached Dwaraka, Sri Krishna and Mother Rukmini appeared as Sri Ram and gave a wonderful darshan to Hanuman. Sri Hanuman, with great devotion and joy, offered them worship and returned to Kadali Vanam. Hanuman knew perfectly well that at that time, it was Sri Krishna who was residing in Dwaraka and Sri Rama had lived in Ayodhya thousands of years back. But he also knew that Sri Krishna was none other than Sri Rama, his beloved deity and he wished to have his darshan in that form. To fulfill the wish of his dearest devotee, Sri Krishna assumed Sri Rama's form - this was possible because he was a Purnavatara (the Lord himself in human form).

Amsa Avatara is a descent of God in human form, where he only partially manifests some of His power in order to fulfill a particular purpose of His. Avesha Avatara is the temporary possession of humans by divine beings to fulfill certain tasks. Of the Bhavas she exhibits, Mother says, "Mother is not manifesting even an infinitesimal part of her spiritual power during the Bhavas-if it were to be manifested as it is, no one would come near. Krishna Bhava is the manifestation of the Parama Purusha aspect and Devi Bhava is the manifestation of the Eternal feminine, the Creatrix, the active principle of the Impersonal Absolute. Mother exhibits both these Bhavas to increase the devotional attitude of the people coming for darshan." By now, I trust the meaning of Bhava darshan would have become clear to you, dear readers; So we shall continue with the biography of Mother, the affable, lovable saint.

At around this time, the divinity manifest in Sudhamani was becoming apparent to everyone in different ways. A huge cobra would be seen moving menacingly on the seashore frightening people during their walks on the beach. During Krishna Bhava, the people told Sudhamani of this and requested her for a solution. The dreaded serpent suddenly appeared at the Darshan. The frightened people ran here and there. Sudhamani caught hold of the serpent and touched its tongue with her own tongue. She then released it and it moved away without harming anyone. From then on, the serpent never appeared on the seashore, and people could resume their walks without any apprehension. To the people who had assembled at the Krishna Bhava that day, it seemed as if their own Kanna (a pet name for little Krishna) who had subdued the Kaaliya serpent in Dwapara Yuga had now come to their rescue. They were wonderstruck at her power.

One is again reminded of Haridasa Thakura, a devotee of Lord Sri Krishna and disciple of Sri Chaitanya Mahaprabhu. He was staying in a cave and had the habit of chanting the names of the Lord 300,000 times daily. There was a poisonous snake in the cave, which emitted such poisonous vapours that people could not even approach the cave. Haridasa, however, seemed unaffected by all this. He did not even seem to be aware of the snake's presence. When Haridasa came out of the cave one day, the people told him of their fears and their inability to come to his cave and have his darshan because of the snake's presence. Haridasa replied that if he had been sincere in chanting the holy names of the Lord, the snake would leave the cave. If that did not happen, he would move to another cave in deference to his follower's requests. As he was speaking, the huge snake having red, yellow and blue stripes and wearing a glittering gem on its head slid out of the cave. The villagers were petrified, but the snake moved away without harming anyone. It was never again seen there. Such was the power Haridasa had gained by chanting daily the Lord's names.

At times other than when she manifested the Krishna Bhava, Sudhamani had to toil as usual in the house hearing all the verbal abuses still heaped on her by her mother and Subhagan, her brother. Subhagan, her elder brother, was especially antagonistic to her. He considered Sudhamani a schizophrenic and created a lot of problems for her. There was an oil lamp kept in the temple and devotees would see to it that it was kept lit throughout the Krishna Bhava. He deliberately broke the oil lamp and spilt all the oil. The devotees were upset, but Sudhamani placed wicks in some seashells that were lying around and lit them without a single drop of oil, and to the surprise of everyone present, the wicks remained alight throughout the Krishna Bhava! Next day, a devotee from a far-off place came to the shrine with an offering of oil-lamps for the shrine! He said he was following instructions received in a dream the previous night.

Some villagers taunted her saying, "Here comes Krishna", and "Hey, where's your flute? Most of the time, she was like an ordinary girl full of an overwhelming love for Krishna. Her parents tried to get her married, but she drove away the prospective suitors by being rude to them or frightening them in different ways. An astrologer who saw her horoscope told Sudhamani's parents to put thoughts of her marriage out of their heads; he told them that it was the horoscope of a 'Mahatma - a great soul'.

One wealthy villager teased Sudhamani saying that she was a crazy girl and suffered from emotional hysteria, because she sang and danced and pretended to be Krishna. He laughed saying that he would give money to her father to see to it that she got married to someone-that would put an end to all her drama! Sudhamani went to her house and collapsed in front of her deity Krishna, crying. She questioned him thus: "Is this the reward I get for being devoted to you and shedding all my tears for you, O Krishna? All these people want me to lead a self-centered life just like them. Won't you grant protection to this little one who incessantly thinks of you? Am I always to be subject to pain and ridicule?"

Meanwhile, the villager who had taunted her went fishing. He and his friends made a particularly large catch that day. Some of his friends were trying to tell him that he should not have taunted Sudhamani. They were about to get off at Parayakadavu and he was laughing saying, "See what happened because I teased that girl? We got a bigger catch than usual." Suddenly he said, "Why don't we go to Neendakara? We can sell the catch for a higher price than at Parayakadavu." So they went out into the sea again. They had almost reached Neendakara when the sea suddenly turned rough - the waves rose menacingly high and despite the fishermen's efforts, their boat overturned and was completely destroyed. Their entire catch was gone. Only they somehow managed to reach the shore safely. The wealthy fisherman's best boat and prized catch were gone. He was inconsolable and repented for his nasty behaviour. He was made to realize that he should never taunt a true devotee of the Lord, as the Lord is the protector of his devotees and does not tolerate any insults directed at his devotees.

Once during Krishna Bhava, Sudhamani had told her father. "My devotees will come from all over the world and some of them will settle here permanently. You'll have to face many obstacles, but do not be afraid. Everything you need shall come to you unasked. Give part of what you receive in charity. This will become a great spiritual center. This little one will travel around the world many times. Although you may have to suffer a lot in the near future, God will always bless you and provide for your needs. Your relatives and some villagers will hate you, but in time, they'll become your friends. Thousands of my devotees will become like your own children." Sugunanandan was astonished. His little daughter who had never even gone up to Cape Comorin (Kanyakumari) 200 kms south of Parayakadavu would go around the world in the future? Thousands of people were going to come to Idamannel-Where on earth would they stay? He dismissed those words, not paying attention to them. Later, when his daughter had become a world-revered saint, the truth contained in those words was brought home to him.

The rationalist movement:

Meanwhile, some of the villagers formed a 'Rationalist movement committed to the removal of blind beliefs'. They rounded up a group of 1000 youth from 13 coastal villages, intending to put an end to Sudhamani's Krishna Bhava. This group persecuted her and Sugunanandan in various ways. They lodged a complaint with the police that something fishy was going on at the Bhava Darshan. A police party came once to investigate, but found nothing untoward. There was just a group of people singing Bhajans and Kirtanas. Later, some people spoke to Sudhamani about their problems. Sudhamani told the policemen that they could arrest her if they wished to; she could at least meditate in peace at the police station. Here, the group of rationalists and the villagers gave her no time to meditate. The policemen, having found nothing fishy and impressed by her calm demeanour, went back. A few days later, another police officer who came for investigation found that he was overcome by a sense of peace and quiet at the darshan. He too went back, saying that the rationalist's charges were baseless. Now, the rationalists ordered two rowdies to catch hold of the mother at the darshan, and frighten her into admitting that her spiritual moods were not genuine. At the Bhava Darshan, they never got the courage to do so. The group then called a sorcerer (a black magician), and he came with the ash got from the body of a charred cobra. He came wanting to test her power, for anybody who received the ash was sure to die. Sudhamani calmly applied it on her body. The sorcerer was sure that she would have convulsions and die, but nothing happened. The treacherous group then, through someone, gave her milk mixed with poison hoping she'd die; Sudhamani drank the milk. Looking directly at the people responsible for this, she vomited in their direction. She was not harmed. Remember Mira Bai, the famous saint and poetess, a devotee of Krishna, who was similarly saved, when the Rana (the King and her husband) gave her milk laced with poison? This only shows that God never fails to protect his devotees when they are subject to torture and humiliation and harassment.

Some of the devotees would call Sudhamani to their houses and arrange a Bhajan and prayer session. The so-called rationalists would gather near their houses and taunt them. Tired of this, the devotees begged her to show them something that would stop them from harassing her and her devotees. Sudhamani smiled and suddenly a great orb of light appeared in the sky, passed through the doors of the house, then moved slowly up into the sky and disappeared. All of them were stunned and most of them stopped harassing her after that.

Forget the rationalists - Even her own brother and group of cousins did not spare her from ridicule and criticism. Sudhamani, meanwhile, cherished an intense desire to have the Darshan of the Supreme Power in the form of the Universal Mother Devi. She had had darshans of Krishna many times and at times of Krishna Bhava, she felt so identified with him that she felt she became him. But now her yearning was to experience the Supreme Power in the form of the Divine Mother who was absolute compassion. It was always the Divine Mother who interceded, with love and compassion, on the devotees' behalf. She used to become immersed in Devi Sadhana, always meditating and calling out to the Divine Mother, "Amma, when can I have your Darshan? Amma, will you not show pity on this hapless child of yours?" Her sole mantra at that time became 'Amma'. She would not take a single step forward without saying Amma. She was oblivious to her physical state. When in deep meditation, snakes could be seen coiling around her body. A flock of parrots (dear to the Devi) would keep vigil near her and tears would flow from their eyes whenever she shed tears for the Divine Mother. When she was living outside in the open (her brother had thrown her out of the house by then), dogs, cats, cows, snakes, goats, squirrels, pigeons and eagles kept her company. They loved being near her. The parrots and pigeons would dance in front of her spreading their wings when she sang to the Divine Mother. She had nursed two small fledglings that had fallen out of an eagle's nest. They grew healthy and strong and always circled overhead during Krishna Bhava. They were a source of great attraction because Garuda is the vehicle of Lord Vishnu (Krishna). The devotee's faith in her divine nature increased. The cows would walk up to Sudhamani and raise their legs inviting Sudhamani to drink their milk. Sudhamani would directly drink the cow's milk. The animals took more care of her than her own family did! Sometimes for months together, she subsisted only on Thulasi leaves and water during this period of Devi Sadhana. Any other cooked food would make her vomit. She cared little for her body and some kind ladies amongst her devotees would personally bathe her and clean her when they found her all muddy, meditating standing knee-deep in the backwaters.

Once when her yearning was very intense, she beheld a great reddish orb of light, which came closer and from it emerged the enchanting form of Devi, the universal Mother, who gave her a beautiful smile. She turned into pure effulgence and Sudhamani felt the light entering her. She soon started manifesting the 'Devi Bhava' along with the Krishna Bhava. People felt amazed at this new occurrence and did not understand initially. Later on, Mother would explain that at times of Krishna Bhava, she felt a supreme detachment – a speciality of Sri Krishna who was fully involved in everything that was happening around him, yet was fully detached. As the Divine Mother, during Devi Bhava, Sudhamani would experience an overwhelming compassion and love that seemed to embrace every creature and all the living beings around her, She could relate to everyone with so much empathy that every single person felt her waves of compassion enveloping them when she embraced them. As the mother, she gave darshan to everyone – men, women, children, old and young, rich and poor, needy and the distressed, with no distinction of caste, creed, colour or status. Whether it was the poor people on the streets or from the slums, or whether it was the rich and influential business people or presidents or prime ministers, they received the same motherly embrace from her. With just a hug, she could transform the lives of people. One is reminded of Sri Chaitanya Mahaprabhu, whose power of compassion was so great that with just a compassionate glance or a warm embrace, he could induce people into chanting the 'Hare Krishna Mahamantra'. His method of preaching was simple. He would just hug anyone he saw on the street and that person would be infused with Krishna Consciousness.

Even if people did not experience solutions to their problems, they recognized an immediate change in their attitudes and perspectives. Where before they had felt as if they had to carry a big load in their chests because of the immense sufferings and intensity of sorrows they had to face in life, they now felt a lightness in their chests as if the weight in their chests had been removed. They felt more confident and courageous and more abler to face any hardship. More than anything else, they felt their hearts opening out in compassion to everybody else around them. Amma kindled in every heart a desire to be of service to those who are less fortunate than themselves. Trust and faith and absolute devotion to the Divine Mother and Father of the universe, and love and compassion taking the form of service to others - She preaches this kind of pure love as the religion that will make the world a better and easier place to live in.

So many wonderful things were taking place in the devotees' lives, but ironically, her own family did not recognize the divinity in her. They put it down to her being possessed by Krishna or Devi a few times a week. At other times, she was just an ordinary girl born to serve them and face their taunts and abuse. They did not feel her state of abidance in God-Consciousness, like the devotees who came from far and wide did. Subhagan, her elder brother hatched a terrible plan with his cousins to get rid of Sudhamani once and for all. To him and a few others who thought like him, Sudhamani was a schizophrenic who was bringing shame on the family by singing and dancing and creating a big drama in the form of Bhava Darshans. One day, he somehow managed to take Sudhamani far away from home and took her to a room in her cousin's house and along with his cousins threatened to kill her if she did not stop all the melodrama. His cousin drew out a knife and tried to stab her; he couldn't do that for he felt an excruciating pain in his own chest and fell down writhing in pain. Damayanti had rushed there by then and forced open the door of the room. The cousin had to be admitted to the hospital. He was in a delirious condition and Sudhamani, bearing no animosity towards him fed him with her own hands at the hospital. Genuinely repentant, he begged forgiveness from Sudhamani for having tried to murder her. He later died after having vomited blood. God never excuses those who insult or torment his devotees. Subhagan continued his habit of harassing the devotees who came to visit Sudhamani. He was struck by a severe form of the dreaded disease elephantiasis and lost his mental balance. A few weeks later, he committed suicide. Consoling her father and mother, Sudhamani told them that he had suffered the consequences of his evil actions, but that he would be reborn later as Kasturi's (her sister) son and he would be a good human being and a devotee of the Lord in that birth. True to her words, Sivan, who was born to Kasturi 3 years later was devoted to the Lord right from his childhood and started meditation and prayers at a very early age.

Meanwhile, Sugunanandan had to face a lot of ridicule and some people alleged that he had murdered his own son. Though it was proved that Subhagan's death was a suicide, people taunted Sugunanandan. Unable to bear all this agony, he cried out to the Divine Mother when she was in Devi Bhava and angrily said that Devi should go away from his daughter's body, as he wanted Sudhamani to get married and lead a normal life. Sudhamani laughed and said that if Devi went away, his daughter would die. Sugunanandan persisted in repeating the same till Sudhamani (in Devi Bhava) said, "Devi will go away - Here, take your daughter back." Sudhamani suddenly fell down lifeless. There was no pulse or heartbeat. Many tried to revive her, but she was truly dead. Everyone cried in deep distress and said that Sudhamani was dead because of the grave error committed by Sugunanandan. Sugunanandan was overcome by remorse and begged forgiveness and requested that his daughter be brought back to life. For eight hours, nothing happened. Sugunanandan kept weeping and repeating his request, when all of a sudden, Sudhamani stirred and got up in Krishna Bhava (Sugunanandan was a devotee of Krishna) and told him: "Without Shakti, there can be no Krishna." Deeply grateful and thankful that Sudhamani had been restored to life; Sugunanandan never doubted his daughter's divinity again. He gave up all idea of getting her married and as far as was possible, saw to it that the people who were against them did not harass her.

People having witnessed her go through terrible ordeals during her childhood, and later seen her subject to harassments of so many kinds by so many others, wondered how she could be so equipoised and calm when such verbal abuse was being heaped on her. To which Sudhamani replied that it mattered little to her who admired her or who harassed her; all children were the same to her. To the question of how she could remain so devoted to God despite the immense hardships she had to face, she replied that her life only proved that it was possible to realize God even under the worst possible circumstances.

Birth and growth of the formal ashram:

In 1976, a youth called Unnikrishnan came from Alappad to visit the Holy Mother. He was very interested in spirituality and he would wander from place to place, hardly spending any time with his family or friends. Once he met Mother, however, he had no wish to go away from her. He wished to stay there and continue his meditation and spiritual practices under her guidance. Mother put him in charge of the temple worship at the small shrine and hall they had been given by Sugunanandan for the Bhava Darshan purposes. He performed daily worship at the shrine and recited the Lalita Sahasranama stotram (a sacred mantra consisting of recitation of the thousand divine names of the Mother) daily as instructed by Mother.

Soon after, a group of youth from Haripad and the neighbouring towns (20 km or so from, Vallickavu, where the Idamannel property was) inspired by the mother's personality and all-embracing love and ideals of the Mother, came to her and requested her to guide them in their spiritual quest. Their names were Sree Kumar, Ramesh Rao, Venugopal, Ramakrishnan and Balagopalan (Balu, who is now known as Swami Amritaswroopananda Puri). Sugunanandan had not objected to the Bhava Darshan, but he did not want anyone coming and staying near the Mother, for he had three other daughters to be married off, and people would talk nonsense if he allowed young men to stay near the house. So all these spiritual seekers were allowed to see Mother for only some time during the day and then they had to go back to their villages.

Another college student who came to be near Mother was harassed by Sugunanandan and he requested Mother to direct him to a place where he could continue his spiritual practices without any tension. The holy Mother told him to go to Thiruvannamalai, the abode of the holy saint Sri Ramana Maharishi, and observe a vow of silence for 41 days. Before leaving, the student asked Mother as to how it would be possible for them to start an Ashram when Sugunanandan was so hostile. Mother assured him that everything would become alright after his return from Thiruvannamalai. There, he would meet a few of her children from other countries, who were anxiously waiting to see her. They would come to Vallickavu and help in setting up the Ashram. She also told him that the day was not far off when Sugunanandan would welcome all of them with love and affection. The student went to Thiruvannamalai and stayed in a cave on the sacred hill, Arunachala. On the third day, faint with hunger, he called out, "Amma" and fell down in exhaustion. He felt someone massaging his forehead and opened his eyes and saw the smiling Holy Mother who had appeared for a few seconds before him. He was thrilled with the experience. At the same time, miles away in Vallickavu, the Mother had suddenly called out, "My Son!" and turning to a devotee had said that her son was starving and she had to see him immediately. After that incident, the student never had any problem for getting food. Someone or the other would always provide him with food.

He met an Australian woman called Gayatri and a native of Reunion Island called Madhusudhana (foreigners following Indian meditation practices sometimes changed their names to Indian names. Now, after initiation, he is known as Prematma Chaitanya). He spoke to them of he Mother and showed them her photograph. They felt a strong stream of love binding them together and felt that they were all the Holy Mother's children. Gayatri had a spiritual experience the moment she saw the photograph. She saw a flash of light and discerned the living form of Mother in that light. Suddenly, a cry rose within her from the depths of her heart - 'Amma, Amma, Amma!' All thoughts subsided and she remained in a kind of trance for 20 minutes. She decided to go to Vallickavu to meet the Mother. There was an American devotee called Nealu, whose spiritual master had been a disciple of Sri Ramana Maharishi. He was bedridden most of the time, suffering from acute pain in the stomach and spine, not able to sit or walk for more than a few moments. Madhusudhana introduced Nealu, who offered him the use of his spiritual master's cottage for observing the vow of silence. Another devotee of Ramana Maharishi called Ganga (from France) also expressed a desire to see the Holy Mother. After the student had observed 41 days of silence, he and Nealu went to Vallickavu. Nealu spent 4 days at Vallickavu. One evening at the end of Devi Bhava, he was standing with folded palms gazing at the Holy mother. All of a sudden, he saw her physical form disappear and become an expanding radiance that spread and enveloped everything visible. The expansive light suddenly contracted into a blazing pinpoint of dazzling light and Nealu felt that the light had entered him. That experience caused him to decide to spend the rest of his life serving the Holy Mother and imbibe her teachings. He returned to Thiruvannamalai, settled his affairs there and came back to settle permanently with the Holy Mother. The Holy Mother told him that he did not have an inch of land that was her own and if they desired to stay there, they had to ask Sugunanandan to provide them some place to stay. By God's grace, Sugunanandan suddenly agreed to give a small piece of land, where he built them a small hut of woven coconut palm leaves. It measured 9 by 18 feet. One corner of the hut was used as a kitchen, and Nealu, Madhu, Balu, Gayatri and Ganga became the first residents of the informally started Ashram. Madhu collected all the existing commentaries on the Bhagavad Gita and translated them into French and carried them with him to the French Island of Re-Union. There, he built a beautiful Ashram dedicated to the Holy Mother, and helped many aspirants to follow the spiritual path.

As predicted by the Mother, those who had formerly been antagonistic slowly started changing and becoming friendly. The weddings of Sugunanandan's three other daughters were arranged and within a couple of years, Mother had helped Sugunanandan to get them all married and settled. Now,

Sugunanandan did not object to the Brahmacharis coming and settling at the Ashram. There were no facilities at the Ashram and the residents sometimes had to manage with just one set of clothing that they had. Food was scarce, and whatever little was received was shared equally by all of them. When some of them complained, Mother told them that spiritual aspirants should not hanker too much after material comforts. She told them to trust God and God would definitely provide for their needs. True to her words, whenever there was a dire necessity for grains or food or clothing, some devotee or the other (who did not even know of the situation at the ashram) would miraculously appear with whatever was needed. Amazed at this, the residents learnt to follow Amma's words that their sole refuge was God and He would provide for them. Commenting on the austere circumstances in which they had to live, Amma told them that if they could withstand this, they could be at home anywhere and would be able to cope with any problems they might have to face later on in life.

The number of residents went on increasing and the idea of formally incorporating as an Ashram was born. Although Mother did not favour the idea originally, she later became convinced of the need for a Government-recognized Spiritual Center. Therefore, on 6th May, 1981, with a view to preserve and propagate the teachings and principles of the Holy Mother, the Mata Amritanandamayi Math and Mission Trust was formally registered under the Travancore - Cochin State Literary and Charitable Act of 1955, at Kollam, Kerala, South India. One of her Brahmacharin sons had given her the name Matha Amritanandamayi and as the name befit her as the Mother of Immortal Bliss, she officially adopted the name Matha Amritanandamayi.

One of her Brahmacharin sons, who was interested in reading a lot of spiritual literature, asked the Mother to select a number in a lottery, where the winner would be given a number of spiritual books. Mother told him that he should not crave for anything that was bound to come on its own. Sure enough, within a few days, Nealu came to settle permanently at the Ashram with his library of more than 2000 spiritual books in English and other Indian languages. The Ashram Library thus came into being by God's will and no extra effort on their part. Soon after, a Vedanta Vidyalaya was started on 27th August 1982, to impart traditional Vedantic and Sanskrit language to the Ashram residents. The Mother always stressed that their practices should go beyond a mere reading of the scriptures. Scriptures were like signboards that showed the way to the Spiritual goal - and that God-realization should be their ultimate goal. And more than anything else, she stressed on the importance of the intensity of devotion (Bhakti-Yoga), which would lead them towards their goal.

A great change came over Sugunanandan and Damayanti and the villagers who had harassed Sudhamani. Realising her divinity more definitely now, her pare .ts began to treat the Ashram residents as their own children, showering affection on them. The Holy Mother was very particular about running the Ashram according to the traditions of the holy Gurukulas of Ancient India. The Ashram work was managed by the residents themselves. Each of them had a duty to perform and they maintained the Ashram themselves, cooking, cleaning and tending to the cows etc. Classes on the holy scriptures, Bhajans, Kirtanas and six to eight hours of meditation were a must for all the Brahmacharis. Mother's fame spread far and wide, she travelled widely in the U.S.A and Europe, meeting with all her spiritual children there, enveloping everyone in the warmth of her embrace and unconditional love. A beautiful residential retreat center came into existence in San Francisco, California.

Initially, many families had created a furore over their sons joining the Ashram, alleging that hypnotism was being used to lure their children there. As usual, some miscreants turned this into a big drama, and gave false stories to the newspapers with an intention to malign the Holy Mother. When the Brahmacharis who had come of their own free will and interest in a spiritual way of life saw all this, they were very upset and angry. When they showed these reports to the Mother, she had laughed and said, "To create trouble is the nature of the ignorant. Why should we get hassled? Look at the beautiful roses and the fragrance they exude - and look at what we give them as fertilizer. Just used tea-leaves and cow-dung as manure. Is the manure befitting the fragrance and beauty of the roses? Likewise, impediments and obstacles are the fertilizers that make us grow stronger spiritually. They will help our hearts blossom fully. So, do not worry about the others who harass us. Pray to God to lead them on the right path. Those who are opposing us today will turn into devotees tomorrow."

Just as she had predicted, the miscreants and rationalists accepting failure, retreated one by one. The committee of Blind Beliefs, unable to prove even a single allegation it had made against the Mother, was dissolved. The Mother and her disciples, finally free of all the harassment, could now concentrate fully on a beautiful blend of spiritual and humanitarian services to uplift and relieve thousands of suffering people. Accordingly, many projects were started to help the poor and needy, the orphans, destitute women, the abandoned elderly people etc. We shall learn more about all these later. Now, I shall bring to you a collection of the experiences of a few people who have had some interesting and amazing incidents happening to them after hearing about or meeting or sometimes even without having heard of the Mother. There are thousands of such incidents, but we can talk of only a few because of space constraints.

Experiences of people:

People who have come for Mother's Darshan or those who have just heard about her and thought about her have had astonishing experiences which have given them a glimpse of the divinity that exists behind the seemingly simple motherly façade she shows to everyone.

(1) Dr. Shrivastava, a scientific officer at the Bhabha Atomic Research Center in Mumbai, writes about his experience with the Mother. In his own words: "During my student days, I had studied accounts of the life of Shri Chaitanya Mahaprabhu which vividly described the flow of divine love from his lips, from his face, and from his actions, when he used to utter the Holy names of the Lord. For many years, I had aspired to see someone with that intense devotion. I met many saints, admirable and worthy of respect, but I failed to find the intensity of radiant bliss I was seeking.

However, when I met Mata Amritanandamayi and heard her songs, even though I could not fully understand the words, I knew I had found what I was seeking. Just by sitting beside her, I could feel the spiritual current one experiences in deep meditation. Her address of the Supreme Power by various names reveals different aspects of the Infinite kaleiodoscopically. Her simple explanations to complex questions show the clarity of her vision of reality. Her spontaneous words impart wings to one's intuition, which enable one to fly to the world of inner light where there are no doubts.

Even in this age of hypocrisy, the number of dedicated seekers is not small, but complete dissolution in Universal love, which Matha Amritanandamayi manifests, is an extremely rare phenomenon."

(2) Ottoor Unni Namboodiripadam: Ottoor Unni Namboodiripad was a well-known poet and Sanskrit scholar in Kerala. He was an authority on Srimad Bhagavatam. His beautiful poems praising Lord Sri Krishna were famous throughout India. Krishna devotees simply loved his poems. He had received titles and awards, both from central and State Governments. He was utterly devoted to the Lord of Guruvayoor, Sri Krishna. A song he wrote 25 years before the Holy Mother's incarnation on earth proved to be very prophetic as we shall see. The song was:

When will I hear the auspicious names of Kanna sounding in my ears?

And upon hearing them, when will my hair stand on end

And when will I be totally immersed in tears?

Being immersed in tears, when will I become pure?

And in that state of absolute purity,

When will I sing his names spontaneously?

And as I sing in ecstasy,

When will I forget the earth and the sky?

And forgetting everything, when will I dance in utter devotion?

And as I dance, will my steps sweep the stains from the stage of the world?

And in that playful dance in which I sweep all the stains away,

I will cry out loud, and through that cry,

Will my purity be sent in the eight directions?

And when the play has been enacted

When will I fall at last into my Mother's lap?

And lying on my Mother's lap, when will I sleep blissfully?

As I sleep, when will I dream of the beautiful form of Sri Krishna

Who dwells within my heart?

And as I wake up, when will I see Sri Krishna,

The enchanter of the world?

Ottoor first met Mother in 1983, during her 30th birthday celebrations. He had had a spontaneous desire to meet her when he heard about her for the first time. He strongly felt that Amma was the divine incarnation of the Supreme Goddess and also of Sri Krishna, his Ishta Devata - his beloved deity. In the presence of Amma, the 85-year old Ottoor became like a two year old child constantly craving the attention and continuous care of his mother. He started composing poems on Mother and asked her permission before doing anything. Mother called him 'Unni Kanna, meaning Baby Krishna' with great affection. He would say he felt energetic just by being near Mother. He lived permanently at the Ashram and used to say that his life was fulfilled only after meeting Mother. He felt that God had not abandoned him as he felt that he was now living in God's presence. He used to keep regretting that he could not enjoy Sri Krishna's pastimes during Dwapara Yuga, or be with Chaitanya Mahaprabhu, the divine incarnation of Radha-Krishna. He did not feel like that any longer as he perceived and felt that Amma was all of them!

Ottoor became very ill in 1989. His greatest wish was to breathe his last in the lap of the Divine Mother. And it did happen that Mother fulfilled his last wish. She knew when his soul would leave his body, and was with him then. His head on her lap and his eyes looking adoringly at Mother's face, he breathed his last as Mother gently closed his eyelids. This kind incarnation of the Divine Mother thus fulfilled Ottoor's last wish and everyone was reminded of the lines of the poem he had written about 31 years back:

And when the play has been enacted, when will I fall at last into my Mother's lap?

And lying on my Mother's lap, when will I sleep blissfully?

(3) Dr. Veena Raj, a devotee of Amma and a homoepathic practitioner in Chennai, describes a wonderful experience she had at one of Amma's darshans. She had a strong desire to garland Amma at one of the darshans. At Vallickavu, she was finally given an opportunity and she was waiting with garland in hand. As she watched Amma coming down the stairs, she was suddenly aware of a continuous flow of light coming from Amma, touching her heart and flowing back to Amma again. This phenomenon continued as Amma came nearer and nearer.

As the doctor garlanded Amma and tried to place the garland neatly on her shoulders she felt her hands sinking into what felt like cottonwool. She did not feel anything solid at all, and then everything seemed to blank out. She could not see Amma or the crowd around her. She felt Amma's hug and a few seconds later, everything came into focus. She could see Amma moving towards the next devotee, and spotting her garland on her neck she became aware that she had finally been able to offer a flower garland to Amma. Later, in a dream, she saw Amma as Devi, dressed in a red sari. When she asked if she could touch her feet, Amma, Amma hugged Veena Raj and told her that her child's place was in her heart. At the next darshan, the doctor was amazed to find Amma in Devi Bhava, wearing the same kind of resplendent red sari as she had seen in her dream. At that Darshan, the doctor was full of tension as there were a lot of problems causing her anxiety and worry. As Amma glanced at her, she felt enveloped by a warmth that instantly dissipated all the worries and anxiety that had been bothering her. From that moment onwards, the doctor felt a transformation in her attitude towards life and could face any problem with courage and confidence, as the comforting warmth and protection of Amma seemed to become a part of her life. She, her husband and her family always look to Amma for guidance, sure that all answers rest within Amma.

(4) My own experience: To each person, any spiritual experience he or she has holds a special significance. It might not necessarily ignite everyone's interest, but it will certainly strike a chord in the heart of people who wish to share their experiences to show that ordinary people too experience the extraordinary Grace of God in various ways, sometimes so strange that it leaves one overwhelmed and stunned for a very long time. I am an ordinary housewife, living an ordinary life as millions of other housewives are doing. I had nurtured an ambition of being a writer more than 20 years ago, but somewhere along the way, the wish had got pushed into some deep recess of my mind, with seemingly no possibility of it ever

rising to the surface again. But certain events happened in quick succession, which showed me that God had not forgotten! I love reading about the life-histories of saints and other spiritual literature about God and his incarnations, his Lilas etc. This gives one courage and peace of mind, which helps one forget the different kinds of traumatic experiences one generally goes through in life. It was no different in my case, and I used to immerse and forget myself while reading about the saints and their lives. In January, I had Amma's Darshan, while she was visiting Chennai. At the meeting I felt nothing very special, except that I felt here was a very warm and friendly person; but within a couple of days, I felt light and experienced a sense of freedom the likes of which I had never experienced before. It was as if a weight had been lifted off my chest. Within a couple of days, I received a photograph of Sri Chaitanya Mahaprabhu and his associates as a gift from ISKCON for having conducted classes for children in their Bhakta Prahlad School for children. A few days after that, when I was least expecting it, I was given an assignment of writing the biographies of Sri Chaitanya Mahaprabhu, Srila Prabhupada and Matha Amritanandamayi! Who says God does not know what is in the innermost hearts of the devotees? It was an overwhelming Grace that descended unexpectedly, for which I shall remain humbly grateful forever.

Still more amazing was something I experienced while reading through accounts of their lives in detail. I had read in brief about Sri Chaitanya Mahaprabhu and Amma, but for the purpose of writing their biographies in brief, I got a lot more reference material lent by kind friends. There, I was amazed at the similarities in so many incidents that occurred in their lives. So much so, I could immediately relate to Mr. Shrivastava when he says (read the first experience) that he could experience the kind of intensity of devotion of Lord Chaitanya's when he met Amma. I have mentioned a few of the similar incidents in this biography. The only three major differences are that Sri Chaitanya was golden in complexion and had a very delightful and almost pampered life during his childhood, whereas Amma was dark in complexion, belonged to a poor family and suffered intense trauma during her childhood years. Why this had to be so is something only God knows about. Later on, their main methods of preaching had one astounding similarity – they could infuse devotion for God in a person just by a warm embrace. Lord Chaitanya's power was so great that any man he embraced would immediately start chanting the Lord's names and singing and dancing in ecstasy. The only limitation was that as Sri Krishna and Radharani had chosen to appear in the form of a Sannyasi, Lord Chaitanya, certain norms had to be followed. Women could not come near Lord Chaitanya – they would offer worship only from a distance. Looks like the merciful Lord has removed that limitation in the recent years, by appearing in a Mother's form easily accessible to all: men, women, children, old or young, rich or poor, ordinary or famous personalities, with no distinction of class or colour, creed or race have all received her famous embrace. Nobody is denied access to her at her Darshan. I almost feel as if Lord Krishna in the form of the Divine Mother has partially incarnated in the form of this benevolent, compassionate saint and is extending Grace and blessings to all. Of course, this is my personal intuitive feeling and I do not expect everyone to concur with this, for every spiritual experience is intensely individual. I can only humbly thank God for this wonderful experience of Grace.

(5) How Amma cured Dattan, the Leper: Dattan hailed from Perumpally near Kayamkulam in Kerala. At a very young age, he had become affected with leprosy. As he grew up, the disease took a toll on his body. He could hardly see and his eyes had become like slits. The hair on his body had fallen out. There were wounds all over his body, with pus and blood oozing out from them. A foul smell emanated from the wounds in his body. His clothes stuck to his body and started to stink because of the pus. His relatives had thrown him out of the house years back and he led a miserable life for no one treated him with affection. He was not allowed to travel in buses; People would not come near him and shrank back in disgust if they suddenly came across him. He had no hope left in life, that is, until he heard about the Holy Amma of Vallickavu. He went to visit her on a Bhava Darshan day. The others would not allow him inside and shouted at him and asked him to go away. But the Holy Mother called him in and treated him as affectionately as she did the others. Over the next few meetings, Mother would pour pots of water on him; she would draw out the blood and pus from his sorely infected wounds with her own mouth. To people, it was a terrifying and blood-curdling sight. Some people would vomit and some would faint on seeing this. Her disciples were worried that something would happen to Amma as Dattan was so badly affected with the disease. Amma would only say, "Can I abandon my child? I see only his heart and not his body. Who else is there to take care of him?" Dattan cried unabashedly as he received a warmth and affection that had been lacking all his life. Within a few months, all his wounds healed. Mother's saliva was the only medicine. He could see again and the hair on his head grew back. He could wear clean, dry clothes now that no pus or blood oozed out of his body. Only the scars from the disease that had afflicted him remained, but his mind and heart were healed and filled with peace and gratitude. People started talking to him again and he felt like a human being again. He remains eternally grateful to Amma for curing him of his disease and also for the affection he received from her.

One is reminded of an incident in Sri Chaitanya Mahaprabhu's life wherein he cured a leper, Vasudeva by name. Vasudeva had oozing sores all over his body, and he did not want to go near the saint because of that. He had only wanted to offer worship from a distance. But the compassionate saint just walked up to him and embraced him with a lot of affection and love. Vasudeva had become fully cured in an instant and had got back his original handsome features. Because of his benevolence, Sri Chaitanya had got the name, 'Vasudevamritaprada', meaning 'the giver of nectar to Vasudeva' - the nectar of good health and life! This was about 500 years ago. Today, Amma has given a similar lease of health and life to someone who could not even dream or imagine he would be cured. Aren't the powers of saints amazing?

(6) There was an ardent devotee of Lord Krishna by name Bhargavi Amma. One night, Lord Krishna appeared to her in a dream and said, "You are burning me up." Bhargavi Amma did not understand what the dream meant, till she attended Mother's Darshan at Krishna Bhava time. Amma told her, "You have locked me up in a cupboard, so you are burning me up." Bhargavi Amma, amazed to hear the same words spoken by Krishna in her dream coming from Amma's mouth suddenly realized the meaning of the words. She used to offer worship regularly to a picture of Krishna, which had been with her for many years. She visited her daughter once and had kept the picture locked in a cupboard, to protect it from insects. On her return, she had forgotten to retrieve the picture from the cupboard. Now, she realized the mistake and begging forgiveness, she kept the picture in the original place at the altar. Today, she is firmly convinced that her beloved deity Krishna and Amma are one and the same.

(7) Mother became a small child herself in the company of other children. There was a small child Shyama who suffered from breathing trouble. She had a severe attack once and the doctors at the hospital pronounced her dead. The grandmother of the child, a devotee of Amma, brought the body of the child to the temple, crying inconsolably. At the same moment, Amma, who was singing at a villager's house nearby, stopped the Bhajans abruptly and rushed to the temple. The grandmother begged her to do something. Mother sat with the dead child on her lap and meditated for a long time. The child suddenly came back to life. The grandmother and the others present there bowed before her gratefully and thanked her from the depth of their hearts.

(8) Rukmini Amma lived at Kollam, 35 km from the Ashram. The right side of her body had been paralysed and she was totally bedridden. For years, her husband Achutan Pillai and family members took her to various doctors. She underwent allopathic

and Ayurvedic treatments. Her condition remained the same, and the family gave up hopes of her ever becoming well again.

They heard about Amma and her healing powers and went to the Ashram. Rukmini Amma was carried on a chair by two strong men. Mother blessed her, gave her sacred ash as 'prasad' and sent her home; she did not talk about her illness or condition at all. The family, disappointed, returned to their house. Rukmini Amma was again being carried into the house when, suddenly, something incredible happened. Rukmini Amma pushed aside her attendants, got up from her chair and walked into the house! The amazed family became ardent devotees of Amma. Any person who saw the agile and active Rukmini Amma later found it hard to believe that she had been completely bedridden with paralysis once upon a time.

(9) Neelambaran, a pious man, devoted to the Holy Mother was a very poor man. Though hardly able to make both ends meet, he would somehow manage to come for Darshan with a flower garland offering to the Mother. Once, he was going through particularly hard times and was talking to the other villagers about his difficulties as he was ploughing a field. The other workers jeered at him when he said, "Today, I don't even have a single paise to buy food." They mocked at him and said, "That girl in Vallickavu (meaning, the Holy Mother) will give you money. Keep waiting for that." Neelambaran felt distressed, as they had teased him about his devotion to Amma. He said nothing. After a few minutes, a very small girl came walking towards Neelambaran, gave him a 20 - rupee note and walked away. When the others asked him who the girl was or whether she was returning some money she had borrowed, Neelambaran had no answer as he too was wondering who the girl was. The next day, when Neelambaran went to see Mother, Amma asked him, "Did the Mother Goddess give a 20 - rupee note to you yesterday? My child, it was Mother who came to give you the money." Neelambaran wept like a child, overwhelmed by her Grace and affection. Needless to say, nobody troubled him afterwards. Such is the Holy Mother's help rendered to devotees, at times of distress and pain.

(10) Puvampuzha Swami was a well-known Swamiji in a village near Kollam. Having heard that Amma had the power of Krishna and Devi, he decided to test her spiritual powers. He entered the temple, having made a Sankalpa (a decision) that if she really had the power of Krishna in her, she would recite a verse from the Bhagavad Gita at their meeting and he would then accept that she was a genuine spiritual master. The Swamiji entered the temple and told Amma that he had wanted to come earlier, but was unable to do so, as his mother had passed away a few days back. The Mother immediately said, "That which is not never comes into being, and that which is, never ceases to exist. Forget not this great truth." Hearing this, the Swamiji was overwhelmed, for Mother's words were an exact translation of the 16th verse of Chapter 2 of Bhagavad Gita. Overcome with awe, he became her devotee.

(11) A devotee called Chandramati regularly came to the Ashram. Once, while she was visiting, Amma, who was receiving the devotees suddenly became very motionless and appeared to be in a state of Samadhi. The devotees waited. After a few minutes, she opened her eyes, looked at Chandramati and said - "Your grandson died some time ago. But the anguished cry of his mother took Amma to her. The child has just come back to life." Nobody, including Chandramati could understand what had happened. Later, it came to be known that at that exact time when Amma suddenly went into Samadhi, Chandramati's 6-year old grandson had suddenly become very ill at his house and had died before medical help could be rendered. His mother Nalini, who was also an ardent devotee of Amma, had called out in deep pain to Amma saying, "Is this the fruit of my devotion to you? Did you have to take my only child away from me?" As she was saying this, a blaze of lightning had flashed near the boy, and he had suddenly come back to life. It was obvious that

Amma had heard the cry of the devotee in distress and had helped the child immediately. Everyone was amazed at Amma's power.

There are many incidents that prove Amma's divinity and the immense power that she wields. But for lack of space and my own limited knowledge of the vastness of her reach and Grace, they cannot be written about here. But, as her devotees have experienced, Amma reaches out to every devotee in a way that is significant and unique. As her disciples say, she hears and answers the sincere prayers of every devotee. She has brought back to life people declared dead from snake-bites, set right so many problems her devotees were facing, blessed people who have been issueless for years with children having divine qualities. She and her dedicated band of disciples have organized 'homas' for world peace and prosperity. 'Matruvani', a wonderful magazine brought out by the Ashram, carries Amma's message of love and spirituality to thousands all over the world. Despite her awesome powers, Amma adopts a very down-to-earth manner and exhibits simple behaviour that endears her to everyone. Everyone experiences a sense of comfort with her. The Ashram routine is very strict and all the Brahmacharis and Brahmacharinis manage the day-to-day activities of the Ashram by themselves. Here, Amma teaches everyone how to practice what she preaches. She does not hesitate to carry sackfuls of sand when any construction activity is going on. She waters the plants herself, helps out in the Kitchen work and teaches people how to behave and work in a sincere manner. For the residents, any work, however complicated, becomes easier to handle with Amma's help and direction. When they see Amma doing manual work herself (she would even clean the toilets herself), they become inspired to work harder. Work that would have taken hours to finish gets done within no time at all, as all the residents of the Ashram participate enthusiastically. Mother would personally serve tea and snacks to the residents at work. She would relieve their tension by relating jokes and making humorous comments. Truly, they all felt that the Ashram was their real home, and Amma was their real mother.

People's perception of Amma:

Each person connects with Amma in his or her own way. This depends on their level of understanding and frame of mind. In the words of Swami Amritaswarupananda (Balu, who has been with the Mother even before the formal start of the Ashram) who has written AMMA-A BIOGRAPHY, Amma is like Mother Earth who bears everything patiently, protecting and nurturing even the people who show scant respect for her. He talks of the people, who, according to their level of understanding give voice to their feeling about Amma in different ways. A person whose intellect is at a very gross level would say, "Amma has extraordinary powers and can cure incurable diseases by a mere touch or look and can solve all your problems and fulfill all your desires. A person whose intellect is at a more subtle level would say, "The Holy Mother can bestow on you many psychic powers. She is a master in telepathy and clairvoyance. All the eight mystic powers are under her sway." A spiritual seeker would probably say, "Amma is the goal to be realized by a spiritual aspirant. She helps true seekers cross the ocean of transmigration. Her nature is bondless compassion and love. She is a veritable witness to the truths expressed in the Vedas and all the scriptural texts of the world. She is a perfect Master and a great Mother."

A person following Bhakti Yoga (the path of devotion) sees all the aspects of Supreme devotion manifesting unimpeded in Mother, like people have observed Sri Chaitanya's ecstatic devotional moods. A Jnana Yogi (follower of the path of knowledge) perceives a perfect knower of the self when he hears her speak of the great truths in a simple and direct way. To a Karma Yogin (follower of the path of action), Amma is the perfect and Supreme among Karma Yogins. Swami Amritaswarupananda says that if one observed without prejudice, one could clearly comprehend that the Holy Mother is an integration of all these. Which is why, any person, illiterate or literate, rich or poor, ordinary or extraordinary can all connect with Amma in their own way. Truly, she is Mother to all her children spread all over the globe. She rejects no one, and treats everyone with love and affection, instructing them in accordance with their mental maturity and need. And all the while, to people who call her God, she only says humbly. "Who is Mother to bless anyone? I am not doing anything. It is God who does everything while appearing to do nothing." Some feel that Amma is a channel for God's manifestation of limitless love and compassion and inexhaustible power and energy. Amma remains detached and unruffled whether people are praising her, blaming her or ridiculing her. Truly, only an enlightened soul can be like this. Her sole aim is to turn all people towards the spiritual path of surrender and love of God.

Many are the charitable institutions she has founded and which are being ably managed by her disciples and devotees all over the world. Mata Amritanandamayi Math's (M.A. Maths) free housing project called Amrita Kuteeram aims to house the slum residents in multi-storeyed flats. A few projects like this have been completed successfully in collaboration with the central and state Governments. The latest and most massive undertaking of this project is the Ajanta Nagar Slum Rehabilitation project. In a phased manner, the project aims to house 10,000 families, presently living in slum areas in thatched huts, in concrete spacious houses with kitchen, toilet and bathroom. The flats are being built with earthquake-proof material (based on experience gained in building homes in Latur and other earthquake-prone areas), in collaboration with the Maharashtra State Government and the Central Government through the Pimpri - Chinchwad Corporation. Amma wishes that even the poorest of the poor should be helped to lead a decent life with at least minimum basic facilities made available. Many are the educational institutions she has started all over India. The Amrita Maha Vidyalayas offer the best in educational

4

facilities and latest technological know-how in various fields of education. On May 15th, 2004, the Amrita-ISRO-Cognizant Satellite-based Education and Network program was launched. This brings together government, industry and university core competencies in a synergistic relation that will use the potential of satellite, information technology, web and networking for education and research across educational institutions under the Amrita University. Experts in one campus can interact with students and researchers in many campuses via the satellite. Amma, expressing joy at the successful launch of the program, talked of how science and technology raised the standard of life. Communication between people all over the world had become much easier because of the machines. At the same time, communication between hearts was necessary to bring the peoples of the world really close together. Amma narrated humorously the story of a super computer that responded instantaneously to different complicated questions on science, Maths and other subjects. But when a small boy asked, "How are you doing?" Its screen drew a blank! Amma thus pointed out in a gentle, unimitable manner the necessity for exploring the inner self too, with as much interest as one pays while exploring the outer world, and coming up with fantastic inventions and discoveries.

Amma has set up hospitals for the poor and needy, homes for the aged, homes for the orphans and destitutes. 'Amma's Kitchens' in many places offer food to the starving and hungry people. It is not possible to mention in more detail about her and her disciples social service and humanitarian projects all over the world, for they are so numerous that it would be beyond the scope of this book.

However, the reader can have an idea of the massive scope of operations the different Amrita institutions are handling. At Amma's 50th birthday celebrations held at Cochin during September 24th-27th, a broad outline was given by the co-ordinators about the Math's programmes. They included:

1) Strengthening of M.A.Math's diverse on-going humanitarian and social-service projects,

2) Conducting 108 free marriages,

3) Eye-donation pledge by 25,000 Amrita Sevaks,

4) Inauguration of a legal cell of 1008 lawyers-Amrita lawyer's Forum, who will offer their services free to the needy,

5) Launching of 100,000 free homes for the destitute homeless over the next ten years,

6) Announcement of Amrita Keerthi Awards-State and National level for outstanding contributors to the revival of Indian culture and Vedic tradition.

Some other charitable homes run by the math are 'Krupa Sagar', a hospice for terminally ill cancer patients, 'Anbu Illam', an old age home; it has also launched an Amrita free meal scheme for feeding 5000 poor people every week at the Brahmasthanam temples. Other institutions the Math runs are, the Amrita Institutes of medical science and technology, advanced computers, pharmaceutical sciences, industrial training centers, Sanskrit Higher Secondary schools, Vedanta Vidyalayams, speech and hearing institutes, Ayurveda research and production centers etc.

How far and wide Amma's waves of compassion have reached can be seen when one sees how people from all over India and the world gathered together for her 50th birthday celebrations. His Excellency, The President of India, Sri. A.P.J. Kalam presided over a mega youth meet for peace and also a business leaders/C.E.O. Summit. The other participants included the Vice-President of India Sri Shekawat and the Honourable Deputy Prime Minister, Sri. L.K. Advani and other outstanding personalities and dignitaries from all over the world. An interfaith meeting of spiritual and religious leaders from all over India and the world was held. An international conference on the Empowerment of women was held. Amma stresses on the importance of empowering women in all fields. Cultural performances from all countries of the world and all Indian States were held. Amma's satsangs, bhajans and darshan on all four days re-energised and rejuvenated all the people gathered there. There were artistic presentations by the finest entertainers from the six continents. There were exhibitions featuring the latest scientific and medical discoveries from all over the world.

From a simple village girl in Kerala, today, Amma has risen to the stature of a compassionate saint revered by people all over the world. It leaves one wondering who or what this phenomenon called Amma is! From the poorest of the poor to the rich and famous achievers, all people become like little children in her presence and yearn for her embrace. Most people see facets of their beloved deity in her. Some believe she is the Divine Mother herself in human form. Speaking for myself, I feel she is a great Mahatma who is an embodiment of divine qualities of patience, pure love, compassion and tolerance and really feel blessed to have had her darshan. Whatever I have been able to bring forth in this biography is very little-based on books written about her and the experiences of a few devotees. I might not even have skimmed the surface of the vast expanse and fathomless depths that are hidden within the seemingly simple, motherly frame.

The Brahmacharis and Brahmacharinis of her Ashram, who have been with her for years, still find it difficult to label or categorize Amma. For as they discover new facets to her each day they spend in her company, they must be feeling she is infinity itself! I leave it to you, dear reader, to form your own opinion of this loveable, compassionate, 'Hugging Saint' of our times.

For it is said that Amma connects with each of her children in a special, unique way. And as she herself says, "People all over the world are my children." And binding everyone together with a mother's unconditional love, she is trying to bring peace, love, compassion and harmony into the world. Let us pray that with God's Grace, her compassionate resolve to bring love and kindness and peace in the world will meet with resounding success and the world will become a peaceful, safe place to dwell in.

Amma has embraced and blessed and consoled more than 30 million people throughout the world. The humanitarian services of her Maths spread all over India and the world have attracted worldwide-attention. Amma has addressed the Parliament of World Religions in Chicago, The United Nations in New York and the Global Peace Initiatives of women religious and spiritual leaders conducted at the UN in Geneva. There, she was awarded the 2002 Gandhi-King Award for non-violence. Amma answers every question in an unimitable, earthy style, full of a mother's love and with the wisdom of a true spiritual master. The most profound, spiritual truths are presented in such a manner that even a child can understand what she is saying. According to her, spirituality is just learning to live as simply and beautifully as possible, constantly in tune with our inner selves. Being spiritual is not about being someone special, it is just about being truly humble all the time and accepting everything that comes our way, whether good or bad with equanimity, reposing complete faith in God and surrendering to God completely.

Spiritual truths are brought out beautifully by simple stories that Amma loves to relate. Many years ago, the world was in a very sorry state. People were cruel and wicked. Poverty was so prevalent that many did not have anything to eat. A lot of fighting always went on. Many felt helpless in the face of such misery. The people of the three worlds namely, the demi-gods, humans and the demons (asuras), met and decided to approach Brahma, the creator of the Universe. They went to him and requested him to give them a solution to end the misery in the world.

Lord Brahma was in a state of deep meditation; he opened his eyes for a second, and said "Da!" and closed his eyes and started meditating again. The demi-gods, humans and the asuras scratched their heads in confusion. Just Da? What in the universe did it mean? They went back to their worlds, wondering about the significance of the word 'Da'. The demi-gods reached heaven, their abode, and saw the dancing apsaras, the celestials singing beautifully, delightful spreads of the most delicious dishes, lovely flowering plants and trees laden with fruit adding to the scenic splendour. Heaven was still the same, full of ways to fulfill the pleasures of the senses. They suddenly realized what their Lord and master must have meant. 'Da' meant 'Dama' (self-control). He wanted them to exercise control over their senses.

The humans returned to earth and saw the sorry state that it was in. There were people so poor that they did not have enough money for even one full meal a day. On the other hand, there were people so rich that they had enough wealth for the succeeding three or four generations of their families. It flashed to them that when Lord Brahma had said 'Da' he must have meant 'Daanam-charity'. It was a wonderful solution to alleviate the poverty of people. If people who had more than what they required, gave enough to people who had nothing, everyone would get a decent meal. Nobody need suffer from hunger or poverty again.

The asuras also pondered over the meaning of the word, 'Da'. They were always planning wars against the demi-gods or launching attacks on the humans, thereby troubling everyone. Lord Brahma must have meant 'Daya-compassion' when he said 'Da'. He was their creator, he knew how cruel and wicked they were. He must have told them to develop compassion so that they could ensure peace in the universe. Three sets of people - and three different interpretations of the word 'Da'. Were they wrong? No, definitely not. Their faith in their Lord's words was so great that they could never go wrong in interpreting them. They had the faith that Lord Brahma would give them a solution to end their miserable state of existence and their faith had not been in vain. His Grace had shown them all the right path and they set to work to translate the advice into action. Soon, the universe started to become a much better place to live in. Dear readers, how wonderful it would be if everyone in the universe with full faith in God, started practicing these principles

Today, the world is in a very bad state. Chaos, misery, violence, hunger, abuse abound in every corner of the globe. What better time than now to start practicing the principles of Dharma (righteousness), Daya, Daanam and Dama? It would surely ensure a peaceful and lovely universe. Amma also always stresses on the same sound values, for ensuring a war-free, strife-free, abuse-free, poverty-free and evil-free good world for all eternity. May God's and Amma's Grace help to turn this beautiful vision into a living reality!

SAINT RAMANA MAHARISHI

India is well known for its many saints and sages who have appeared with unfailing regularity to grace her hallowed land. They have always provided solace to the suffering millions, lifting people out of their depression, helping them to face life with confidence and courage by leading them forward on the path of self-realization.

One such saint was Sri Ramana Maharishi and he was referred to as the 'gentle sage of Arunachala'. His mere glance was enough to remove the pain and sorrow of his devotees. His silence spoke more eloquently than words. His presence was enough to send people into a state of indescribable bliss, and they would feel at peace ever afterwards. Dear Reader, let us go on a journey together to discover what made this saint so revered all over India and the world.

In the town of Tiruchuzhi in Tamil Nadu, there lived a couple Sundaram Iyer and Alagammal. On the festival day of 'Arudra Darshan - the sight of Lord Shiva' on 30th December 1879, Alagammal gave birth to her second son, a bonny baby. A blind lady who was assisting at the delivery, suddenly perceived a dazzling flash of light for a second as the baby cried and announced its entry into the world. The couple named the child Venkataraman.

Venkataraman was a well built, healthy boy; he was very naughty too. He was more interested in swimming, wrestling etc. Studies took a backseat, as he enjoyed playing pranks on others and generally enjoying himself. Once, he had broken into the locked house of a lawyer taken some important papers and distributed them to the people on the streets saying they were advertisements for a play! Venkataraman's father was so angry that he ordered that Venkataraman should be given only a loin-cloth to wear and that his head should be shaved completely and that he should go without food for a day. Years later, Venkataraman (by then the Holy Saint, Sri Ramana Maharishi) almost seemed to be re-enacting the punishment as he had his head shaved completely, began wearing just a loin-cloth and stayed without food for long periods.

Venkataraman had another very fond hobby – he loved to sleep most of the time. In fact, he loved it so much and it was so impossible to wake him up that people had named him 'Kumbhakarna', Ravana's brother, who slept for six months a year and had to be woken up with loud trumpeting and noisy drums! Some of Venkataramana's enemies, who he had had fights with earlier, would beat him up when he was asleep to take their revenge, as they were confident that even that would not wake him up! They had no guts to do that when he was awake, as he was a very strong boy. He would wake up on his own after long periods. Many years later, people would wonder, whether on those occasions, Venkataraman had been immersed in a state of Samadhi, and that was why it had been so impossible to wake him up on such occasions!

Venkataraman's father died when he was twelve. He and his elder brother were sent to their paternal uncle's house in Madurai, where he was enrolled in The American Mission High School.

When he was 16 years old, he was sitting in a room in his uncle's house, when a sudden fear of death seized him. Initially frightened, he later decided to face the fear head-on and lay down like a corpse, trying to hold his breath and pretending to be as dead as possible. He tried to distance himself from thoughts of body and mind. In an instant, he felt himself as pure awareness and was conscious of being a witness to everything. He felt he was the pure spirit and had transcended the mind and body. This kind of instant self-realization happens very rarely, even amongst saints. From that moment onwards, he became disinterested in the worldly life he led with his family and friends. He became introspective and deeply absorbed in thoughts of the self. He would visit the Madurai Meenakshi temple and stand in front of the idol, tears streaming down his face, as he seemed to be engulfed in great joy. When he saw the idols of the saints, he was overcome with emotion as he recalled facets of their lives he had read about in the 'Peria Puranam', which had the life-stories of the 63 Nayanmars, the Saivite Saints. These two incidents proved to be a turning point in his life. He cherished a desire to go to Thiruvannamalai and the Arunachala hills. The name Arunachala had a strange fascination for him ever since his childhood. Now, the intensity of longing would not allow him any peace of mind. He would suddenly lapse into a meditative state at school or at home or wherever he happened to be at that time. His family and teachers could not understand his moods of absorption. His brother was taunted him saying that he should go to the forests. Once, he could not concentrate on his homework and pushed his books aside and sitting cross-legged started to meditate. His brother was angry that he was making no effort to study and thereby become capable of earning a living, teased him saying, "What is the use of all this to such a one?" meaning a real sadhak should have no use for all the comforts that a home-life offered. This statement made a deep impression on Ramana's heart and he also felt that if he was to embark on a path of renunciation, he had no right to live in comfort at home at the same time. He decided to leave his family and home and go to Arunachala. He wrote a letter to his uncle and brother, telling them not to search for him. Taking just three rupees, which he thought would be sufficient for his journey, he walked away from home. He had five rupees given to him by his brother to pay his college fees. The remaining two rupees, he placed it along with the note he left behind, wherein he said that he was going to seek out his real 'Father'.

He travelled by train for some distance, walked several hours when his money ran out. On the second night, he reached a Shiva temple at Aranyaninallur. He sat down in the hall and immediately there was a brilliant flash of light that brightened the temple in the dark hours of the night. At the house of one Krishna Bhagavathar, the lady of the house gave him some food to eat and also a packet of sweets. She was very happy that she could feed someone on that day, as it happened to be Gokulashtami, the birthday of Baby Krishna. He exchanged his earrings for a sum of 4 rupees and proceeded on his journey again. Finally, on September 1, 1896, he reached Thiruvannamalai. He ran to the temple of Arunachaleeshwara, a form of Lord Shiva and said simply, "Father, I have come." His eyes filled with tears as he gazed at the sacred Arunachala Hills.

Legend of Arunachala:

Arunachala is one of the oldest and most sacred places in India. Bhagavan Ramana Maharishi had declared that it is the Heart of the earth, the spiritual center of the world. Sri Shankara spoke of the Arunachala hills as the legendary Mount Meru. The Skanda Purana declares, "Of all, Arunachala is the most sacred. It is the heart of the world. Know it to be the secret and most sacred heart-center of Lord Shiva." Many saints have meditated there. To this day, it is said and Bhagavan has confirmed that many Siddhas (sages with supernatural powers) dwell in its caves. It is said that they are seen as lights moving about in the night.

A hymn to Arunachala goes:

Ocean of nectar, full of Grace.

Engulfing the universe in thy splendour;

O Arunachala, the Supreme itself

Be thou the Sun

And open the lotus of my heart in bliss.

According to the legend, Lord Vishnu represents the ego or individuality, Lord Brahma the mentality and Lord Shiva, the Paramatma or the Spirit. Shiva once appeared as an infinite column of light to settle a dispute between Vishnu and Brahma. The column of light was so dazzling and impossible to look upon, both Brahma and Vishnu prayed to Shiva to take a more benevolent and accessible form so that all beings could realize the goal of life by worshipping Him. Shiva accordingly took the form of Arunachala Hill, declaring. "As the moon derives its light from the Sun, so other holy places will derive their sanctity from Arunachala. This is the only place where I have taken this form for the benefit of devotees who wish to worship me and attain illumination. Arunachala is 'Aum" itself. I will appear on the summit of this hill every year at Kartika, in the form of a peace-giving beacon." Thousands of devotees do 'Pradakshina' (circumambulating the hill), like a living garland, slowly moving along the eight-mile trail that surrounds the base of the Holy hill.

We shall come back to the life-story of the saint after reading about the wonderful legend about Arunachala. After reaching Thiruvannamalai, Venkataramana removed the sacred thread he wore, had his head completely shaved and started living like a Sannyasi. He wore only a loincloth. He sat like a statue with hardly any movement. He never spoke for months together and always appeared to be absorbed in deep meditation. Sometimes, naughty boys pelted him with stones to see if he was a statue or someone real. There was an underground chamber called "Patala Lingam", below the thousand-pillared hall of the temple where he stayed. It was unclean and dark and full of mosquitoes and ants. He shifted to this place to escape the harassment of the boys who threw stones at him. The atmosphere there did not put him off. Despite being bitten severely, he continued to sit and meditate in that place. Later, some sadhus forcibly lifted him from here and took him to a temple dedicated to Lord Subramaniyam (Muruga). He remained deep in meditation there also. Daily, abhishekas with water, milk, sugar and various holy mixtures were performed to the idol. A Swamiji observing a vow of silence also lived in the temple. He would collect this mixture and offer it to Venkataramana. Venkataramana subsisted only on this prasadam. The temple priest noticed this and started giving him pure milk to drink.

After a few days, he moved to the Gurumoortham temple. There, a young Malayali Sadhu named Palanisami started serving him, as he could sense some kind of divinity in Venkataramana, who had achieved God-realization by then and could counsel the thousands of people coming for his darshan. Many people found solutions to their problems and doubts. Many offerings were made to him-fruit and food offerings made by the devotees were distributed as prasad - Venkataramana would eat very little. The rest, he shared with everyone around him. Palanisami brought a lot of books on philosophy. Bhagawan's spiritual experiences helped him to absorb the essence of all the teachings at a glance. He learnt Sanskrit, Malayalam and Telugu by reading books brought to him in those languages. He would do this for the benefit of Palanisami, who wanted to know the essence of the teachings presented in those books

In 1899, Venkataramana moved to the Virupaksha cave on the Arunachala hill. He was here for 17 years. A 13th century saint called Virupaksha had lived and been buried there. The cave was shaped like the sacred syllable 'Aum'. The sound of 'Aum' seems to be echoing from the cave, according to some people. There were many wild animals near the cave but Venkataramana was not afraid of them. In his presence, the wild beasts would become calm and start playing with each other. On such occasions, his devotees would get scared, but Venkataramana would calm them down.

A Sanskrit scholar named Ganapati Shastri came to see Venkataramana and had discussions with him on various spiritual topics. Astonished at the way all his queries and doubts were miraculously cleared in the simplest of terms, he gave Venkataramana the name Bhagwan Ramana Maharishi, the name by which he is well-known all over the world today. Meanwhile, his uncle, mother and brother had finally found out where he stayed and had tried many times to take him back to Madurai.

At that time, he was not speaking with anyone, so he had written on a slip of paper a message to his mother. It read, "Whatever is destined not to happen, will not happen, try as you may. Whatever is destined to happen will happen, do what you may to prevent it. The best course is, therefore, to remain silent." His mother and brother had gone back, but later, in 1916, they came to stay with him. He looked after them well, but gave them no preferential treatment. Many devotees would come to visit him and his mother started caring for them as if they were her own children.

His mother had sudden glimpses of his divinity. Once, she saw him disappear in front of her own eyes. There was only an effulgent column of light where he was seated. She was terrified and thought that he had left for his heavenly abode and was pleased when he appeared again in his usual human form. Ramana Maharishi lived for years on the food he got when he went on his rounds of 'Bhiksha' (requests for food). Later, his disciples did the same. They requested him to compose a special song so that they could sing that and be identified as Ramana's devotees. That was when Sri Ramana composed 'Akshara Manimalai', a song in praise of Arunachala. He composed all the 108 verses in it while doing 'Pradakshina' of the Arunachala hill. When the devotees sang that and repeated the sacred name 'Arunachala Shiva' the householders would come out and offer them food. Ramana Maharishi would say that having to beg for food was one way of remaining humble always. Some days, a very meager amount of food would be collected and there would not be enough for him and his disciples. On those days, he would grind the food collected into a fine paste, mix it with a lot of hot water and the gruel would be shared equally amongst themselves. They did not have money to buy even salt or spices. On days when they had next to nothing, Ramana Maharishi would humourously say that they were observing 'Ekadashi (the day of fasting). On some days, they would have a variety of food, which they would all share equally. Maharishi would say that it was 'Dwadashi' (the day of breaking the fast).

Around this time, a widow named Echammal, who had lost her husband and both her children, all within a space of few years, came to meet the Maharishi. She had been to various places of pilgrimage and was seeking relief from the immense sorrow and grief that had enveloped her whole being. But nothing had given her the peace of mind she was seeking. As she stood in front of Ramana Maharishi, no words were spoken, but the limitless compassion that flowed from his eyes lifted the burden of sorrow from her heart. From that day onwards, she cooked a meal for him and his devotees and carried it up the hill on some days or sent it through someone if she could not manage to climb the hill. The very act of service provided solace to her grieving heart. She did this service for the rest of her life even when the Ramana Ashram had come up and the Ashram cooks had begun cooking regularly. Ramana Maharishi always began his meal by eating what Echammal had sent. If the cooks by any chance forgot to serve that first, he would sit silently, refusing to eat till someone realized what had happened and they would rush to serve him the food sent by Echammal first. Such was his affection towards his devotee.

Ramana Maharishi's mother passed away in 1922. A shrine was constructed at the spot where her body had been cremated at the foot of Arunachala Hill. The Ramana Ashram came up there after a few years as the number of devotees increased and a lot of money came in. Slowly, a big prayer hall, a dining hall, office buildings, a bookshop and small houses for devotees started coming up. Ramana's younger brother Nagasundaram was in charge of the committee, which managed the Ashram activities. In the initial stages of building the Ashram, when they were staying in just a couple of small huts, thieves broke into the Ashram and stole whatever they could get their hands on. Ramana Maharishi sat in silence after telling them that they could not hope to get much there, it being an Ashram, and as Sadhus, they had very little material possessions. The thieves, angry that they got very little, beat up Ramana Maharishi and the residents before going away. When the residents, shocked and sad that their master had also got beaten up, asked why he had not let them retaliate or fight with the intruders, he said: "We are Sadhus. We should not give up our Dharma. They are misguided men, ignorant men. Why should we behave like them? If your teeth suddenly bit your tongue, do you knock them out in consequence?" The thieves later got caught by the police and were put in prison.

The Maharishi would always say: "The Lord controls the fate of souls in accordance with their 'Praarabhda Karma'- meaning Paapa (sins) or Punya (merits) acquired in the past births. All the actions that the body is to perform are already decided at the time it comes into existence; the only freedom you have is whether or not to identify yourself with the body."

Maharishi's unique method of initiating his disciples:

Maharishi always initiated his disciples through look and silence. The disciples being initiated could feel Maharishi's luminous, transparent eyes piercing into every corner of their minds, breaking down their thought processes. The disciple would feel strong vibrations and immediately a feeling that the Master had accepted him as his disciple would envelop him. This happened with most of his disciples. People compared Bhagwan's silent initiation 'Mauna Diksha' to Lord Dakshinamurthi's eloquent silence, which would dispel the doubts in the minds of his disciples. The disciples would feel that, henceforth, Bhagwan would guide them in all their endeavors as His Grace had flown into them.

Sri Ramana Maharishi would personally supervise the cooking in the kitchen sometimes. He was very particular about not wasting any foodstuff. Even the peels of vegetables would be used for feeding the cattle. If he spotted any laziness amongst any of his devotees, he would not reprimand them, but would take the task upon himself and do his share of the work also. This served the purpose of teaching them a lesson very well. The concerned person would never again give in to laziness. He would not permit anyone to rise or stand when he entered the Hall. His humility was so great that he told them that if they showed him such respect, they should be doing the same for anyone who entered the hall. He expected no preferential treatment because so many spiritual aspirants considered him their Guru. Even when his health started declining, he refused special diets recommended for him. When someone suggested that he should be given orange juice everyday he refused, saying that unless they could afford to give orange juice to every inmate of the Ashram, the suggestion could not even be considered. According to him, whatever they could afford and prepare, had to be equally shared by everyone present.

Ramana Maharishi's love for animals:

Ramana Maharishi had great affection for all the animals and creatures and birds. A villager had a dream in which he was told to offer his next calf to the Ramana Ashram. He gifted his cow and newly born calf to the Ashram. The calf grew into the famous cow Lakshmi of the Ashram. She would come daily to the Ashram Hall to have her meals, and contentedly settle down near the Maharishi. She was looked after wonderfully by Bhagawan and towards the end of her life, died peacefully as he was holding her in his arms.

Several monkeys would approach Bhagawan and climb onto his couch. He treated all the animals that came to him as if they were humans and called them by the names he gave all of them. Sick animals were brought to the Bhagawan. He would place them next to himself on the couch and treat them till they were well. None of the animals fought or attacked each other. There were squirrels nests on the roof of the old hall. Some baby squirrels, no more than an inch long, dropped onto Bhagawan's sofa. They were red in colour, absolutely tender. People wondered how they were to take care of something so tiny and tender. Bhagawan kept them in the palm of his hand and asked for some cotton. He made a tiny bed of cotton, placed the squirrels in it. He made a wick with a pointed end from cotton, dipped it in

5

milk and squeezed the milk into the squirrels' tiny mouths. He looked after them with great compassion till they grew up and were able to run around. They never ran away, they always ran around him and kept close to him as if he was their real mother!

A badly wounded deer had wandered into the Ashram. The Maharishi held in his arms and comforted it during its last moments and it died peacefully. He built a Samadhi for the deer in his Ashram alongside the samadhis of a few other animals. He would not permit any snakes on the hillside to be killed. He said that they had no right to disturb them in their natural habitats. They did not harm anyone unnecessarily; so they should also not be harmed was his advice to everyone. He would solve disputes between groups of monkeys. He understood their behaviour and they seemed to understand what he spoke to them. They were always well behaved in his presence. The animals who resided in the Ashram and died there were buried in the Ashram compound after funeral rites were performed for them.

Maharishi would talk to the animals as if they were human beings; it always seemed to the onlookers that they could understand and really converse with one another. The idea of 'Samadarshitva' was fully manifest in him-meaning, he saw and treated everyone man or woman, rich or poor, famous or ordinary, animals, birds, insects or any other creatures and trees and plants with equal respect. He would not refer to animals as people generally referred to them saying 'Adu'-meaning 'it' in Tamil. He would refer to them as 'avan', or 'aval'-meaning 'he' or 'she'. He would say, "Who knows which souls are inhabiting these bodies?" The animals would eat out of his hands; he showed them so much concern and affection. Once while climbing a hill, he disturbed a hornet's nest with his leg. The furious hornets attacked his leg. The Maharishi stood still until their fury had abated, accepting it as a punishment for his intrusion!

A few important teachings of Ramana Maharishi:

Sri Ramana Maharishi's teachings were directed towards all people in all walks of life. The eternal principles of 'Sanatana

Dharma', that he always spoke about were explained in such a simple manner that even a child could understand what he was saying. To the seekers who came to him, he would say that the Grace of the Guru was limitless, like an ocean. But if people came to the ocean with only a cup, they would only get a cupful of Grace. The bigger the vessel, more Grace would flow in. What he meant to convey was that the Grace of the Guru would simply flow - unimpeded by any blockage or obstruction - into the hearts of those who opened their hearts out to him.

Ramana Maharishi would often warn his disciples not to get too attached to Siddhis (miraculous powers gained by doing yoga and meditation) because they would be obstacles to the realization of the self. He said that with purity and strength of mind acquired through meditation, it was even possible to talk to God like SriRamakrishna Paramahamsa did. If one required peace of mind, one could only achieve it by a process of self-enquiry. The only Siddhi one should aspire for was realization of the self, because that was the highest Siddhi. To a person who had realized the self, the manifestations of power and knowledge would result on their own accord and be God-given. But whether the powers manifested or not, the true Jnani who is always at perfect peace would not be disturbed by either occurrence.

He said that greedily begging occult powers (Siddhis) from God, who is ready to give Himself who is everything, is like begging worthless stale gruel from a generous natured philanthropist who will readily give everything. So, the only thing to aim for while surrendering to God was God-realization. To everyone, he pointed out that they had to go back to their source, their innermost self and then there would be no problems for them. The only way this would be possible was by a process of self-enquiry and complete surrender to God, Guru or the Self. According to Ramana Maharishi, complete submission to God, Guru or the Self was one and the same.

He would explain that Jnana and Bhakti were essentially the same. The path of Bhakti, devotion or surrendering the ego to a higher power and the path of Jnana, Knowledge were not to be considered two different paths. His explanation was: "The eternal, unbroken, natural state of abiding in the Self is Jnana or Knowledge. To abide in the Self, you must love the Self. Since God is in fact the Self, love of the Self is love of God, and that is Bhakti. Jnana and Bhakti are thus one and the same."

He stressed on the importance of rising above the attachments that arose because of the ego, which always resulted in sorrow. "Turn away from the ego, and turn within towards the eternally blissful self. You'll then be free from all miseries and problems then", he would advise. Many people experienced relief from their problems, physical illness, mental or emotional problems and others simply by being near him during the prayer and meditation sessions in the hall. People became free of their diseases and worries so quickly; it seemed nothing short of a miracle. Many people did not even need to express their problems verbally. Just by visiting him and melting under his all-knowing and compassionate glance, they would return healthier and happier individuals. He would infuse in them a desire towards God-Consciousness and God-realization.

There was a big stone-slab on top of the hill where Ramana Maharishi would sit brushing his teeth. His elderly devotees found it easier to have darshan of him from their houses itself because of this. They could just look up and feel happy, seeing him there. This was very convenient for them as it was very difficult for most of them to climb up the hill, as they were very old. The kind Maharishi thus fulfilled their wish of having his darshan everyday by this kind gesture of his.

Experiences of people:

Nobody could predict how Ramana Maharishi would greet people. Some high and mighty people would not even merit a cursory glance from him, while some seemingly insignificant wanderer coming in would receive his concentrated attention for hours or sometimes days. Once a Swamiji called Pranavananda came to the Ashram. He was so exhausted. He sat on the steps of the temple itself, as he could not even take a step further. Ramana Maharishi came out at once, massaged the Swamiji's feet, although the old Swamiji protested and after he felt better, led him inside.

One lady devotee called Ramani Ammal says: There was magic in Ramana Maharishi's eyes. Each devotee in the packed hall would feel that he was gazing into their eyes. By his look itself, he would make people aware of what meditation was. People would be instantly transported to a state of Samadhi, where they were unaware of their mind and body. They would all experience a feeling of peace. Every single devotee felt the same.

A devotee called Sampurnamma, who did not even know what meditation was, neither was aware of how to stop her mind from thinking, would find that in Bhagwan's presence, not a single thought came to her mind. Her mind would become peaceful and completely clear. She experienced a state of calmness and a deep happiness within her.

Sri Balarama Reddy, a devote says, "Bhagwan's attendants had told me that his body was like a furnace; only when I sat close to him did I realize what they meant. He felt spiritual power emanating from his body like an electric dynamo. I was thrilled to the core of my being."

M.G. Shanmugam, another devotee recalls how one's doubts got automatically cleared in Bhagwan's presence. In a strange and uncanny way, the doubts he had would be expressed in the form of a question by some other devotee present there and Ramana Maharishi would not only answer the question, but also look at Shanmugam and smile conspiratorially as if he was asking him whether he had received his answer. Many people had their doubts cleared similarly, without ever having to express them aloud.

He always had a fathomless look in his eyes as if he was always detached from his body. The powerful aura around him radiated peace and bliss and anyone who sat in the hall felt the full force of it. He would just look kindly and compassionately with that powerful gaze of his which had become world-famous, and the devotee would instantly feel free of any burden or pain that had been bothering him or causing him anguish. Their problems seemed to melt away as he rested his gaze on them.

Sampurnamma, the Ashram cook, had to walk along a jungle path skirting the hill. Bhagawan noticed it once and told her not to be afraid as he was always with her. Once, she and Subbulakshmi, her friend, decided to do pradakshina of the hill and started well before daybreak. There were panthers and snakes and possibly wicked evildoers in the jungle. They began to feel very afraid, but then, suddenly, a blue light appeared in front of them and led them along the path and disappeared only at daybreak. Though it had been an uncanny experience, they realized that they had felt safe with the light.

Another time when they were doing pradakshina, they noticed a man following them. He stopped when they stopped and walked when they walked. They were alarmed and prayed to Lord Arunachaleeshwara to save them. As if reading their thoughts, the man at some distance behind them said loudly, "Yes. Arunachala is our only refuge. It is his light that fills the space. Keep your mind on him constantly." When they turned back in surprise for they had been praying in their minds, the man disappeared into thin air! From then on, they no longer felt afraid as they felt Bhagawan was always protecting them in some form or the other. They however wondered whether the man they saw was Ramana Maharishi or Lord Arunachaleeshwara himself! Thus, Ramana Maharishi seemed to be Arunachala Paramatma in human form to many devotees.

Sri Ramana attains to the spiritual realm:

In 1944, a small growth appeared below the elbow of his left arm. A doctor removed it surgically, but it soon returned, larger and more painful than before. It was diagnosed as a form of cancer. Again and again, the lump was removed, but it kept recurring. The cancer soon spread to his whole body. The Maharishi maintained his daily routine for as long as it was physically possible for him. In 1950, he became very weak and was unable to receive visitors in the hall. He was shifted to a small room with a bathroom, adjoining the hall. The devotees filing past in the hall could have his darshan as they filed past his room. He kept saying that loss of the body was no reason to grieve, but his devotees were inconsolable. When he heard a grieving woman devotee knocking her head against a post outside his room, his sense of humor made him say- "Oh! I thought someone was trying to break a coconut!" The doctors were amazed at the Maharishi's indifference to the pain, as it must have been really hard to bear. But he bore the illness and its consequences remarkably well. He kept assuring everyone that he was not going away, but would always be with them. Some wondered why a saint who cured so many of their diseases should himself have been subject to such a dreaded disease. But the wise said that it was because the Maharishi took upon himself the sicknesses and burdens of those who came to him for relief from their problems. In any case, his body had served its purpose and it was time for it to transcend to the other state. On the evening of April 24th Sri Ramana Maharishi's earthly sojourn in the limiting physical frame came to an end, as a glorious, luminous light shot upwards towards the summit of Arunachala and disappeared. His devotees grieved, but not for long as they felt his spiritual presence even more strongly now. Experiences of many devotees after he left his physical body go to prove that Sri Ramana Maharishi was still with all of them and they would always be inspired, protected and guided by him in all their endeavors.

Experiences of devotees when Sri Ramana Maharishi entered the spiritual realm:

T.M.P. Mahadevan, a devotee says, "The end to the physical body came on April 24, 1950. That evening, the sage gave darshan to everyone. Everyone knew that the end was nearing and they were singing Bhagawan's hymn to Arunachala with the refrain 'Arunachala Shiva'. The sage asked his attendants to make him sit up. He opened his luminous and gracious eyes for a while and smiles as a tear of bliss trickled out from his eyes. At 8.47 P.M., the breathing stopped. There was no spasm, no struggle. At that very moment, a comet moved slowly across the sky, reached the summit of Arunachala and disappeared behind it.

Another devotee, Sri Nambiar says, "Late in the evening, after dinner, my wife, children and I were sitting in the courtyard when suddenly my younger son, Vijayan looked at the sky and said, "Papa, see what is in the sky, a big star?" We all looked up. Somewhere in the western sky was a bright meteor moving at an unusual speed, too slow for a shooting star and too fast to be an aircraft. My intuition was about Bhagwan and I exclaimed, 'It is Bhagawan passing into the spiritual state'."

Monsieur Cartier-Brassen, the French photographer, related an astonishing experience: "It was a most astonishing experience", he said. "I was in the open space in front of my house, when my friends drew my attention to the sky, where I saw a vividly luminous shooting star with a luminous tail unlike any other shooting star I had seen before. It came from the south, reached the top of Arunachala hill and disappeared behind it. Because of its singularity we all guessed its import and then raced to the Ashram only to find that our guess was sadly true. The Master had passed into 'Mahanirvana' at that very minute we had seen the shooting star.

A devotee called Smt. Ramani Ammal in Rajapalyam, saw a blue light rising up in the sky and knew that Bhagawan had left the body. She was so attached to the Bhagawan that she started fasting to starve herself to death. Her brother and sister also started fasting. She had dreams and visions after 5 or 6 days of fasting where she saw Bhagawan seated on Arunachala hill near a tank, with rishis serving him. He looked splendid and gracious. She saw Kamadhenu, the celestial cow and Kalpavriksha, the celestial tree and many other wonderful sights. Bhagawan gave her some prasad and made her eat. She could not refuse his prasad. He told her - "You keep repeating that I have gone away. Where have I gone? I am right here. Look inward. If you look within, I am there." After this dream, Ramani Ammal became convinced that Ramana Maharishi had not left them and that he would be ever-present with them. She broke her fast and was unhappy no longer, as Bhagawan's presence was so definitely felt by all of them.

Yolande Levi, a devotee wrote to New York Arunachala Ashram about a friend of hers in Romania, who was a dedicated doctor earning little. Her husband had left her and she had sunk into depression and was anxious all the time. She read something about Ramana Maharishi in a book about spiritual giants. His name kept coming to her mind though she had read about many other saints too. Yolandi sent Bhagawan's photo to her. As she was about to dose herself with anti-depressant medicines, she looked at the photo that she had come to adore and gave up all her pain and sorrow to the saint in the photograph. She felt at ease and at peace immediately. She quit all her medicines and got courage and strength simply by looking at Bhagawan's eyes in the photograph. That doctor lives in a remote place, knows no English, knows nothing of spiritual teachings or literature. Yet, a sincere call of surrender made in her heart brought Bhagawan's Grace descending on her in a wonderful and unexpected way. Thus prayers made even from miles away get answered with the Grace of a Guru.

Sri Ramana Maharishi used to say of his states of exaltation: "Some power acts through the body of a Jivanmukta (a liberated soul) and uses his body to get work done." He often said, "I am not the body, I am the Self." Though devotees missed his physical presence, they experienced his spiritual presence always with them at the Ashram or elsewhere.

Some final tributes to Ramana Maharishi:

Dalai Lama: The heritage of India is enriched with numberless saints and Yogis. Sage Ramana represents that tradition and his spiritual greatness is guiding millions of people. Such masters light the path and bring solace to suffering humanity.

A prophecy by Sri Muruganar: "Bhagawan's real power will be seen not now, but only a few hundred years after his physical body is no more. But we will not be able to see those days."

So, the simple, yet great saint continues to live and guide his devotees everywhere with his spiritual presence in their hearts. We should all aspire to follow this important teaching of his: He used to say, "Tear aside the veils and see the divine majesty of your own self. Dive inside to find the true treasure of the self, hidden within you. Open your heart and see the world through the eyes of the true self."

SHIRDI SAI BABA

'Sai Baba' - the name that is so dearly loved by millions of people all over India and the world means 'True Mother and Father'. 'Sa' stands for Sachhe (true). 'Aai' means 'Mother' in Marathi, (the language of the Maharashtrians, the state where Shirdi Baba made his appearance), and 'Baba' stands for 'Father'. So, 'Sai Baba' denotes 'True Mother and Father'. As Sai Baba is believed to be an avatar (incarnation) of the Lord, the name is most befitting for this kind and loving saint, who made Shirdi, a small town in Maharashtra, his home. Hence the prefix 'Shirdi' was attached to his name and he became known all over the world as Shirdiwale Sai Baba.

Shirdi Sai Baba endeared himself to people of all religions. Known for his kindness and affection to the downtrodden, the poor and needy, he touched the hearts of millions with his unassuming life-style and humane behaviour that embraced all, regardless of caste, creed, status or colour. His words provided solace to all who came to him for advice and comfort. The miracles that occurred in the lives of all his devotees, were ample proof that he seemed to be all knowing and ever-present anywhere. Calls of distress of sincere devotees were answered even if Sai Baba were physically thousands of miles away. Many people believed that he had divine powers. Some said he was Divinity, God himself in human form.

Sai Baba never called himself God - He would always say, "Allah Maalik Hai" (meaning Allah is the Lord and Master), or "Bhagwan Bhala Karega" (meaning, God will do something good), and "Sabka Maalik Ek Hai" (meaning, There is only one Lord and Master, and he is the same for everyone). He always gave the impression that he was a channel for God's power and attributed all the powers and miracles that people experienced to the Lord's power and Grace. This humble nature of his endeared him to thousands who flocked to him with their problems.

Appearance at Dhoopkede:

Sai Baba's life-story makes wonderful reading. In a small village in Aurangabad district of Maharashtra, a young fakir (sadhu) made his appearance. When he was first noticed, he was sitting under a margosa (neem) tree in 1854. Nobody knew his name or where he had come from. His saintly demeanour and bright eyes attracted many, who wished to know more about him. He disappeared after a few days and nobody knew where he had gone.

Chand Bhai, the Patel (headman) of a village called Dhoopkede was frantically searching for his missing horse. He spotted the young fakir, who asked him what he was searching for. Then, the fakir pointed in a direction beyond a thick hedge and the horse suddenly appeared there. Chand Bhai felt that there was some divine power latent within the boy. Many villagers flocked to him to his wise words and counsel. Once, a marriage procession was making its way from Dhoopkede to Shirdi. The fakir joined the procession. On the outskirts of Shirdi was the famous 'Khandoba' temple. The processionists wanted to offer worship there. As soon as the priest spotted the young fakir, he spontaneously called out, "Welcome to you, O Sai Baba (the true mother and father). Everyone believed that Lord Khandoba himself had made the priest utter those words, and from that day, the young fakir was known as 'Sai Baba'. He made Shirdi his home from then on. It was the year 1858.

There was a dilapidated mosque at Shirdi. Baba made that his home and called it 'Dwarakamayi'. Many villagers, aware of the divine aura that seemed to surround him, gave him the respect due to saintly persons. They came to him with their problems and miraculously all their problems started getting solved by Baba's Grace. In the early days at Shirdi, he would either keep wandering in the jungles or on the outskirts of the village. At other times, he would be found sitting under the neem tree, immersed in deep meditation. His first set of disciples, who instinctively felt that he was a divine saint, were Mahalaspati, the priest. Tatya Kote and a few others including Bayyaji Bai. Bayyaji Bai felt a motherly love towards this saintly young man, and she took upon herself the task of feeding him. She would wander about in search of him in the deep jungle, till she found him seated in meditation under some tree or the other. She would make sure that he took his meal and then return home. It was then that, out of compassion for her determination to see that he was fed even if it meant walking miles in the jungle searching for him, that he made the mosque he called 'Dwarakamayi', his home. (Dwaraka was Lord Sri Krishna's capital city in Dwaparayuga).

A saint called Devidas, living in Shirdi, and another householder saint by name Gangagir, who frequently visited Shirdi, recognized Sai Baba's divinity and told everyone that he (Sai Baba) was no ordinary person, but a divine power in human form and that the soil of Shirdi was blessed to have earned his Grace. Baba grew a big flower-garden with a lot of effort and patience. Today, the Samadhi Mandir of Baba stands in this place.

Baba did not mix or speak with people unless he was questioned or asked advice about something. He wore a long, flowing kafni (robe), and had a length of white cloth on his head. The white cloth was twisted like matted hair and flowed down from the left ear on his back. He wore no shoes or sandals. His seat was a piece of sackcloth. He sat in front of a Dhuni (sacred fire) facing south, to ward off the cold. His sole possessions were a chillum (a pipe). Tobacco, a 'Tumrel' (a tin-pot) and a 'Satka' (short stick), which he always kept with him.

Sai Baba loved lighting lamps. He would borrow oil from the banias (shopkeepers) and light the lamps and keep them burning throughout the night. There was a small girl amongst his group of devotees, who Sai Baba was very fond of. Once, during Deepavali (the festival of lights), the shopkeepers suddenly decided not to give him oil as he did not make any payment for it. The little girl was upset and wondered how they could celebrate Deepavali without lighting lamps. The kind Baba told her not to cry. He put dry wicks in the lamps. He took the tumrel (tin-pot) which had a few drops of oil in it and poured water in it. He drank that water and again filled the tumrel with water. He poured this water into all the lamps and lit them. Amazingly, the wicks lit up with this water and stayed alight throughout the night. Amazes at this, the repentant shopkeepers begged forgiveness from Baba and never refused him oil again.

Many devotes discerned a peculiar characteristic about a piligrimage to Shirdi. Nobody who came to visit Baba at Shirdi could leave without his permission. And if Baba told someone who was intending to stay longer to leave Shirdi, he had to obey immediately. People who disobeyed him always had to face problems later on, as can be seen from a couple of incidents, which will be described here.

(1) Tatya Kote Patil, a devotee of Baba was going in a tonga (horse-cart) to Kopergaon bazaar. He offered pranaams to Baba at the masjid and told him not to leave the village and stop for some time. He told him to take Shama (Madhav Rao Deshpande, another close devotee of his) at least along with him. Not heeding his directions, Tatya set off immediately. Soon, one of the horses became very restless and fell - the tonga met with an accident. Tatya Kote was not hurt, but he was reminded of Sai Baba's advice. This happened twice, before he realized that he must listen to Baba's advice and start only with his permission. He was not hurt on either occasion and attributed this to Baba's Grace. He resolved to pay heed to Baba's advice from then on.

(2) A European gentleman who had come for Baba's darshan was told to leave the next day, and not on the same day as he was intending to. Disregarding this advice, he set off and met with an accident and had to be treated for injuries at the Kopergaon Hospital.

These incidents taught people to listen and act according to Baba's advice. Those who listened were safe and happy and did not meet with any problems.

People wondered why, with all his amazing powers, Baba relied on householders for food. He would visit five houses only everyday, with his begging bowl. Whatever was received, whether little or more, was shared with his disciples. The Baba explained that there was a significance behind the Sannyasis going from house to house requesting for food. The Sannyasis, who turn the minds of the householders Godwards, gave much more than they got, in the form of spiritual instructions. Baba too belonged to this category. Secondly, householders in the process of cooking food invariably incurred a lot of sin, while grinding food, pounding the grains, cleaning and washing vegetables and lighting hearths. A lot of small creatures were unintentionally destroyed. To atone for this, a few processes (yagnas) had been prescribed in the scriptures and shastras. They were: (1) Brahma-yagna (worship of Brahman), (2) Vedadhyayana (study of Vedas), (3) Pitru Yagna (offerings to ancestors, (4) Deva-yagna (offerings to Gods), (5) Bhoota yagna (offerings to other beings) and (6) Manushya Atithi yagna (offerings to men or sudden, unexpected guests and Sannyasis).

With all this, the minds of human beings were gradually cleansed and purified, leading them on a path of self-realization. Baba, by going from house to house, reminded the householders of their sacred duty and the people whose homes he visited were indeed blessed to have been given the opportunity of serving a saint.

Spiritual experiences of devotees of Baba:

(1) Smt. Tarkhad, a great devotee of Baba, had once sent a peda with a friend Sri Mankar who was leaving for Shirdi. As he had informed her of his intention to visit Shirdi just a few minutes before he left, she did not have time to prepare anything to send to Baba as an offering. There was only a peda (milk sweet)

in the house, and she sent that with him. Sri Mankar visited Baba twice at Shirdi, and both the times, Baba asked him what he had got for him. Mankar had forgotten all about the peda and left it behind in his room at the lodgings where he stayed. Baba suddenly said, "Did not Mother (Smt. Tarkhand) send a peda with you when you left?" Mankar suddenly remembered the peda and ran to get it. Baba ate the humble offering with great relish and proved that he accepts all sincere offerings of his devotees, however humble or small the offering might be.

The same Smt. Tarkhand had another wonderful spiritual experience. She was visiting Shirdi and staying at a house there. She was about to have her meals one day, when a dog outside the house started howling with hunger. Before starting her meal, she fed a few pieces of bread to the dog. The dog ate it and went away happily wagging its tail. At Baba's darshan that afternoon, Baba suddenly told Smt. Tarkhand, Mother, "You have fed me so sumptuously today that my life-force has been satisfied. Always act like you have done and this will stand you in good stead. Always take pity on me like this. First give bread to the hungry and then eat yourself. Never forget this." Smt. Tarkhand was very surprised and said, "Baba, how could I have fed you? I myself am dependent on others for my needs." Baba smilingly told her, "I am still belching in satisfaction, after eating that tasty bread you gave me in the morning. The dog whom you fed before your morning meal, is one with me; so also are the other creatures (cats, pigs flies, cows etc) are all one with me. I am roaming in their forms. He, who sees me in all these creatures, is my Beloved. So, abandon the sense of duality and distinction and serve me always like you did today." Hearing this, Smt. Tarkhand's eyes filled with tears and she was too overwhelmed to speak. What Baba was trying to teach through this incident is that one must learn to see God in all beings. Our Upanishads, Gita, Bhagavatam etc., all teach us to perceive God in all creatures. Sai Baba was demonstrating how to put these Upanishadic teachings into practice.

The instances where Baba wrought transformations in many lives are too numerous to mention for lack of space. Only a few can be mentioned here, but they serve in effectively proving the kind of power he had, which he used to help his devotees in distress. He never failed to answer their calls for help.

(2) A Baba devotee, Sri Tilak Bhaskar, talks of a traumatic experience their family had to go through when his daughter, suffering from an attack of Bone TB, in the backbone, lost her power to walk. Doctors at AIIMS, Delhi had talked of a possible chance of recovery after an operation of the backbone. Now, this was very worrying to the family, as the doctors had also told them that this operation was fraught with danger and also had a very, very low success rate. A friend of Bhaskar, very devoted to Shirdi Sai Baba, visited his daughter in hospital and gave her Sai Bhabhuti (sacred ash) brought from Shirdi. That afternoon, his daughter was all smiles and she said that she felt an urge to test her legs, first the left and then the right one. After almost 4 months of no movement in her legs, the girl suddenly started walking again, slowly but surely. This miracle happened soon after she received Baba's prasad., a cure in the form of holy ash. The doctors were amazed and said that only God could have cured her of the miserable condition she had been in. The operation was not necessary any longer as the girl had started walking and would recover fully, slowly and surely. This news spread to everyone at the AIIMS Hospital and many people came to request them to pray for Baba's blessings. The family requested them to pray to Sainath, as he was the one who had performed the miracle. After they went home, it took almost two years for her to completely regain her strength. After she recovered fully, the family went on a thanks-giving piligrimage to Shirdi. The daughter is now a happily married woman, having two children. She fasts every Thursday and visits the Lodhi Road Sai Mandir without fail. She and her family can never forget the miracle that restored strength in her legs. They remain indebted to Baba forever.

(3) A devotee called Prasanna Vadana talks of her nephew, a 5-year old boy who had suffered from a hairline fracture of the knee. The doctors said that he had to be admitted to the hospital for complete bed rest. The family first took him to Baba's temple and applied Udi (sacred ash) on his knee. After two days, when they took him to the hospital, the doctors noticed an improvement in his condition and sent them back with medicines, saying hospitalization would not be necessary, as the fracture seemed to have healed on its own! Baba's Udi had effected the cure!

A devotee of Baba, by name Rekha, talks of her husband's experience. Her husband had been suffering from cancer and he had lapsed into a semi-coma during the treatment. He said that he had seen a triangle in the clouds, and after saying that he lapsed into a deep coma. All her relatives and well-wishers prayed to Baba and applied 'Udi' on his forehead day and night. When the doctors declared him dead, the grieving family members played Sai Bhajans continuously without losing hope. On the third day, her husband opened his eyes and told them that as he was walking on a long path, Baba had suddenly appeared before him and made the sign of 'Aum', and sent him back. The family is ever grateful to Baba, who they call their eternal saviour and who had given Rekha's husband a second lease of life.

A devotee from Assam, Devyani Bhuiyan, had a miscarriage and doctors had told her that she could not have another baby again. She suffered from other health problems as well. Though losing hope, they continued their prayers to Baba. One day, her husband had gone to the Sai Mandir in Lodhi Road, New Delhi. He was sitting on a bench in the temple complex, when an old man, barefoot and in a worn-out Dhoti, came and sat next to him. As he looked very impoverished, Devyani's husband gave him all the cash he had with him in his pocket on that day. The old man had smiled as he told him, "When you have your son, don't forget to come here. Your Baba will be waiting for you." The husband was astonished and did not know what to make of this statement. Meanwhile, Devyani had been suffering from immense pain from pus, and blood was oozing out from ruptured stitches, due to a carelessly conducted gall-bladder operation. She met a devotee of Baba called Guru Ma, who blessed her and told her that Baba would heal her. Within a few days, the stitches healed completely and she was freed from the trauma she was going through. Later, she and her husband were blessed with a baby boy, although the doctors had told them that they would not have another baby. The husband was suddenly reminded of the old man he had met in the temple and realized that he must have been Baba himself. He was amazed and felt blessed to have had Baba's personal darshan. The family worships Sai Baba as their God now.

Sai Baba's devotees all over the world have experienced many more miracles like these. A devotee feels amazed that every time he utters the word 'Aum Sai Ram' as he is travelling anywhere, a car or a vehicle with the words, 'Aum Sai Ram' materializes within a few seconds from somewhere! The devotee has had this experience too many times to dismiss this as mere co-incidence. He thus feels the presence of Baba wherever he is.

Shirdi Sai Baba continues to make his grace and blessings felt in the lives of millions of his devotees by appearing in their dreams or personally appearing in different forms and solving all the problems and relieving the miseries of millions of his devotees. His devotees always adhere to the thought that Baba has ingrained in their minds and hearts-'Sabka Maalik Ek', meaning the Lord of everyone is one and the same, although he might appear in different forms. This helps to foster a feeling of brotherhood, peace and unity amongst his devotees, whichever faith they belong to, all over the world.

Shirdi Sai Baba's devotees at various Baba temples perform a lot of service activities for the poor and under privileged. One of the most important activities is 'Annadhanam'-feeding the poor people and poor children living in the vicinity of the temples, at least once a week, mostly Thursdays. Many schools are run for poor children, by the Sai Charitable organizations. In a place called Gummidipoondi in Tiruvallur district near Chennai, a devotee called Ezhumalai Swami has built a small temple for Shirdi Baba. A report about this temple had appeared in The Hindu paper, which focused on the 76-year old devotee's single-minded determination to make service to humanity his goal, as Shirdi Baba used to advise everyone that service to humanity in any form is service to God. Ezhumalai lives on a pension of just a couple of thousands a month and has a wife, a widowed daughter and two grandchildren to look after, but manages somehow to feed about 400 people, mostly poor children on every Thursday. He also has to buy logs for the continuous burning of 'Dhuni-sacred fire', needs oil for the lamps etc. When asked how he can manage to feed so many poor people, he just smiles and says, "I don't do anything; He (Baba) does everything'. Somehow, every week, as Thursday draws near, devotees and philanthropists give in donations in cash or kind and the feeding program goes on unhindered. Many miracles have taken place here. Ezhumalai's own wife, who could not walk and was not responding to treatment from doctors, was cured by the 'Udi-sacred ashes from the Dhuni'. A tired bullock had collapsed in front of the temple and was refusing to move, but was up and about soon after Ezhumalai had applied Udi on a wound it had from some poisonous bite. A man who had not recovered completely from a snake-bite was suffering from various health problems for almost two years because of that. Soon after he started applying Udi that Ezhumalai gave him, he was completely cured within a few weeks. Full of gratitude, he performed Annadhanam at the temple as thanksgiving. Ezhumalai wants to start a primary school for poor children. From donations received he has started constructing a Kalyana Mandapam. After it is complete, he hopes to rent it out for weddings and functions and use the money for continuing Annadhanam for the poor, and also feeding the Sadhus and Sannyasis who visit the temple. He is confident that Baba will help him in his endeavour. Thus, many sincere devotees like

Ezhumalai are translating Baba's maxim of Service to Mankind into action. Let us pray that this spirit of service and the spirit of unity and brotherhood of man, which Baba has planted in many hearts will continue to grow and be nurtured by the goodwill of God and Baba's Grace, so that peace, oneness and goodness will prevail in the entire universe.

SATHYA SAI BABA OF PUTTAPARTHI

Sathya Sai Baba, who is believed to be a divine incarnation by millions of people all over India and the world, was born on 23rd November 1926, in the early hours of the morning at Puttaparthi, Andhra Pradesh. His parents Pedda Venkappa Raju and Eashwaramma were a pious couple belonging to a Raju (Kshatriya), middle-class family, which had always been a religious family  devoted to God. The family participated in and encouraged music, literature and cultural activities. They belonged to the Bharadwaja Gotra. His great grandfather Kondamma Raju, a scholar of ancient scriptures, had built a temple for Goddess Sathyabhama, Lord Sri Krishna's consort, at Puttaparthi village after the Goddess had appeared to him in a dream. His grandfather Venka Avadhoota had renounced material and worldly attachments for a spiritual way of life. His father, Sri Venkappa Raju was famous for the roles he played from the epics, when plays were staged during festivals and functions. He would lose himself in devotion as he played religious characters on stage.

Birth:

A few days before Sai Baba's birth, strange incidents occurred in his house. The tanpura (stringed instrument) and the mridangam (drums) and other musical instruments played on their own and produced melodious notes on their own without anyone even touching them! Venkappa Raju's mother was an ardent devotee of Lord Sri Sathyanarayana, and Sathyanarayana Pujas were performed regularly at the house. In fact, as Sai Baba was born in the early hours of the morning on November 23rd, Sathyanarayana puja was going on in the house at that very moment. As soon as her mother-in-law gave her the Sathyanarayana prasadam, Eashwarama delivered the baby in the middle of the auspicious Brahma-Muhurtham period. Accordingly, the baby was named Sathyanarayana.

The baby did not cry as soon as he was born like other babies. It had a beaming smile on its face. The blanket on which the baby lay suddenly rocked on its own, and on inspection, a cobra was found coiled under the blanket! The people were frightened, but the snake did not harm anyone and disappeared quietly. Later, as the child's divinity became apparent, people said that he was none other than Ananthapadmanabha (the reclining form of Lord Vishnu on Shesh Nag, the divine seat of the Lord); in a child's form, he was lying down on the cobra, who was Shesh-nag come to provide a soft bed for the baby at its birth!

Her mother-in-law had dreamt of Lord Sathyanarayana in her dreams and had told Eashwaramma to take note of anything unusual happening. Eashwaramma had gone to draw water from the well, when all of a sudden, she saw a blue ball of light gliding towards her. She felt the blue light gliding into her stomach and lost consciousness. The child was born soon thereafter. And, as already noted, musical instruments played of their own accord, and a fragrance of jasmine flowers pervaded the entire house soon after his birth. The child was beautiful, with a mole on the left cheek; even as a child, holy ash (vibhuti) materialized out of his palms mysteriously, whenever he covered his face playfully.

Childhood at Puttaparthi:

Sathyanarayana was an immensely kind, gentle-natured child. He was always concerned about the poor and the needy. He took care of animals and birds in pain. He never teased or troubled animals or birds like some cruel children did. He would tell them also to show kindness to everyone. At a very early age, he used to insist that the family members feed the beggars and poor people in need. There was an elderly lady named Subbamma near his house. He would spend most of his time there and would eat only vegetarian food cooked by her. He would play games with other children on the banks of the River Chitravadi near his village. He loved to sing and dance with them. He loved to worship images of Gods and Goddesses and would teach his friends religious and moral lessons. At the age of ten, he had formed a 'Pandhari Bhajan Mandali', consisting of his group of friends. They all sang devotional songs in praise of Lord Vitthala (Sri Krishna) of Pandharpur.

As he grew into adolescence, he was sent to his sister-in-law's brother's family at Kamlapur. There, he had to help out in household chores like fetching wood, and carrying water in large vessels from a hill, which was quite a distance away from their home. He would help everyone uncomplainingly. Both as a boy and a youth, he used to miraculously produce stationery items, sweets, fruits etc, for his friends. Due to poverty, he had to manage with only one set of uniform. He himself daily washed and ironed it. He used to write poems advertising goods from the local stores in the market area and thus earned a little money to meet his expenses. Later, he was sent to another brother's house at Urvakonda. There also, he had to help out in all the household chores as they were looking after his needs.

Once, he was enjoying himself sitting on a wooden revolving chair in his brother's house, when his sister-in-law's brother scolded him and forced him to get off the chair. Satyanarayana had enigmatically told him, "A day will come when I will sit on such a chair made of silver and you will live to see that day." Seven years later, this prophecy of Satyanarayana came true, when he had attained worldwide fame as Sai Baba, and the Rani of Chincholi presented Baba a silver chair. The relative who had insulted Baba years back was asked to unwrap it at the 'Prashanthi Nilayam Ashram'.

Sathyanarayana would lapse into deep, introspective silences often and would talk philosophy very often and this amazed the villagers. At other times he could be seen laughing, singing and dancing with such gay abandon, that people thought he was possessed by strange spirits. On 23rd May, he was materializing sugar candy, sweets and flower before an amazed audience, when some people complained to his father. Enraged at what he thought was exhibitionism and drama, he ran with a stick in hand, to beat up his son. He yelled at him asking, "Who are you? God, ghost or a lunatic?" Sathyanarayana replied, "I am Sai Baba. I belong to Bharadwaj Gotra. I have come to save you all from danger. Keep your houses clean and pure."

Some people laughed and asked him to prove his divinity then and there. Sathyanarayana asked a person standing in the crowd to give him some jasmine flowers he had with him. He gathered the flowers and scattered them on the ground. To the astonishment of everyone present, the strewn flowers arranged themselves on the ground to form the word 'Sai Baba' in Telugu, Sathya's mother tongue.

In October, Sathyanarayana and his brother were invited by Rama Raju, Chairman of Bellary municipal committee to spend the puja holidays with him. One day, a group of 50-60 people were taken to see the ruins of Hampi. When they all went inside, Sathyanarayana pretended to have a stomach ache and stayed outside the temple. The people who went inside were astonished to see the live image of Sathyanarayana that appeared on the idol of Virupaksha. Someone was sent outside to check if Sathya was still waiting outside. He came back, replying in the affirmative. Seeing Sathya in two places at the same time, some more people became convinced that some form of divine power existed within him. On 20th October, 1940, he renounced his family ties, saying that Maya (illusion) had gone and his devotees were calling him. He had a lot of work to do for the betterment of the world.

Thereafter, he went to the garden of his devotee Anjaneyulu and sat on a rock amidst trees, A crowd assembled to hear him.

He sang the first prayer, teaching all to sing it throughout their lives:

"Manas Bhaj re Guru charanam

Dusthar Bhava-Sagar Taranam"

Meaning, "Meditate in thy mind on the lotus feet of the Guru; this alone can take you across the turbulent sea of worldly existence birth after birth.

A few days later, a photographer who took the photograph of Baba seated next to a big stone. When he developed the picture, he was astonished to find Shirdi Sai Baba's picture in place of the stone, which had been there when he had taken the picture. In many other ways and to many devotees, he proved that he was Shirdi Baba reborn.

A devotee of Shirdi Baba called Sri. M.S. Dixit was convinced that Sathya Sai Baba was a re-incarnation of Shirdi Sai Baba. He had requested Shirdi Baba that he would like to keep watch at the gates of 'Dwaraka Mai'. Sathya Sai Baba fulfilled this devotees' desire in this incarnation by giving him the job of opening and closing the gates at Baba's Whitefield Ashram, 'Brindavan', whenever Baba's car passed through.

Before attaining Mahasamadhi, Shirdi Sai Baba had confided to Abdul Baba, his trusted devotee and companion at Dwaraka Mai (the mosque where Shirdi Baba stayed) that he would be reborn after eight years with the name 'Sathya'. People believe Sathya Sai Baba who was born in 1926, is an avatar of Shirdi Baba. Sathya Sai Baba, talking of a boon Sage Bharadwaja had got from Lord Shiva and Goddess Parvati said that the Sai Avatars are a result of that boon. According to Sathya Sai Baba, Shirdi Baba was an avatar of Lord Shiva. He (Sathya Sai Baba) was a combined avatar of Lord Shiva and Goddess Parvati. He has predicted that the next Sai Avatar, Prema Sai, would be born in Mandya district in Karnataka State in 2022. She would be an avatar of Goddess Parvati. An era of peace and love would prevail upon the earth with the advent of the third avatar. People hope these words should definitely come true and save people from the miserable existence in a world full of strife and violence. People hope that the world will be a better place for their children at least, when: Sathya (truth), Shanti (peace), Dharma (righteousness) and Prema (love) will rule all over the world. As Sathya Sai Baba, like so many other great saints, is propagating all these ideals along with doing numberless humanitarian service activities in society, it is the hope of thousands that his prediction of a world, where the only true religion would be truth and love, will come to pass.

People started believing in his divinity as many had their problems solved after visiting him and having his darshan. A few people were cured of incurable diseases. Many experienced relief from their physical, mental and emotional problems. His fame spread far and wide; many people, including foreigners, who had his darshan in their dreams, were lead to him and became his devotees. Sathya Sai Baba says of the miracles he performs, that they are his visiting cards. He uses them as baits to draw people to him and strengthen their faith in the divine. Later, he directed them towards the path of God-realization, showing them that being God-conscious always is the only goal to be had in life.

Baba's fame grew and on his 25th birthday on 23rd November 1950, the famous Ptashanti Nilayam (Abode of peace) was inaugurated. Now, it is a large township attracting millions of people from all over the world, all through the year. In 1959, a big Banyan tree was planted in a grove behind Prashanti Nilayam. Today, it serves as a Meditation tree under which hundreds of devotees sit and meditate.

In 1961, he installed a marble idol of Shirdi Sai Baba in the famous Nag Sai temple (where Shirdi Baba had appeared as a serpent while worship was being offered to him). On that day, he had declared that he had come to re-establish Dharma in the world.

Slowly and steadily, many educational institutions at Anantapur, Brindavan, Whitefield (near Bangalore), where another of his famous ashrams had come up, Jaipur and Bhopal had come up. Sri Sathya Sai Institute of higher learning, established in 1982 at Prashanti Nilayam, is now a deemed university with Baba as its chancellor.

Baba has launched a movement of 'EHV'-Education in Human Values, in India and all over the world. Sai Seva Samitis have been formed in about 90 countries; all of them are involved in social service activities.

A super-speciality hospital was inaugurated on his birthday 23rd November in 1991. This unique hospital offers absolutely free treatment to the poor, whether it is a kidney transplant, minor or major surgeries or any other affliction. The poor have benefited immensely by this.

The concept of 'Spiritual fraternity' can be seen in action in about 50,000 Sai Service centers all over the world. Everyone, regardless of their status, caste or position, forgets their differences and better themselves through selfless service of the masses. One of the supremely famous teachings of Baba is, "There is only one caste, the caste of humanity. There is only one religion, the religion of love. There is only one language, the language of the heart. There is only one God - He is omnipresent."

His devotees have pledged to serve him as God through service to the poor and needy in their own countries (in villages, slums in cities, unhealthy human habitations etc). They are guided by a common code of conduct and their staunch faith in the unity of all religions. They are all propagators of Sathya, Dharma, Shanti and Prema - all values needed for the spiritual regeneration in society, for ushering in a more peaceful world. He always advocates that the way to reach God is through selfless service; 'Manav Seva, Madhav Seva'-that is, service to mankind is service to God. All the people in all the institutions he has founded all over the world strictly follow this doctrine of his.

Although he has declared that He is God in human form, he does not tell any devotee to stop worshipping the form of the deity he is devoted to. He tells them to continue worshipping any form of God of their faith. He only emphasizes that they should follow the path of righteousness and love and always be ready to help others, never hurt or harm others. He prevails upon the rich to share what they have in excess with the poor and needy so that the deprived also can experience some form of comfort and warmth in their lives. He upholds the sanctity, dignity and unity of all religions in the world, by giving a place of honor to all the religious symbols of all great religions of the world in the official symbol of his mission - 'Aum' of Hinduism; 'Cross' of Christianity; 'moon and star' of Islam; 'fire symbol' of Zoroastrianism;'Wheel' of Buddhism and the pillar of religions erected by Baba in the center of all of them. He encourages his devotees to sing the glories of the names of Sri Rama, Sri Krishna. Pandurang, Hanuman, Allah, Christ, Gurus, Mahavir, Buddha, Zoroaster, etc., that is, the chosen Gods of all religions. Festivals of all faiths are celebrated with great enthusiasm in his Ashram. Thus, an attempt to bring together people of all religions under the commom platform of Truth and Love, is being encouraged and attempted by all devotees of Baba by his Grace on them

Service activities:

The 'Sri Sathya Sai Seva organization has three wings: (1) Spiritual, (2) Service and (3) Educational.

(1) Spiritual Wing: 'Singing Bhajans' is one of the prime activities of this wing. All the functions, festival celebrations are begun with Bhajans. The main purpose of this is to help people realize God by consciously chanting his names and singing songs in his glory. Constantly thinking of God and singing about Him is one of the recommended processes for reaching God in this age. Baba says that when Bhakti (devotion) and Jnana (knowledge) take firm root in man, he sees God in everyone and this realization prompts him to do selfless service to his fellow-beings, as it is Seva (Service) to God. 'Seva' is said to be the ultimate 'Sadhana'. All Sai centers and Samitis organize Bhajans in the houses of devotees as well as at public gatherings. During these sessions, hymns and songs in praise of Gods and Goddesses of the Hindu religion, and of all other religions are sung. Many people, sense the presence of Baba in mysterious ways, whenever the Bhajan sessions are held. He has assured his devotees that he will be present wherever the Bhajans are being held. His devotees do 'Nagar Sankirtana' (on the lines of Sri Chatanya Mahaprabhu, who would dance and sing the glories of the Lord on the streets) in their towns also. In the early hours of the morning, separate rows of men and women devotees walk through the streets, chanting the names of God melodiously. The spiritual wing is also engaged in imparting spiritual training to adults and children and teachers to produce spiritual literature.

(2) Service Wing: Devotees attached to this wing, conduct various service activities which include health and hygiene, rural service activities, medical camps, visits to hospitals, Narayan Seva (programs for feeding the poor on massive scales), Shramdan (service to the handicapped), blood donations etc.

Baba says, "Every act of service, however small, is service to the Divine. Therefore, serve fellow-beings who are in need." His devotees have adopted around 6000 villages in many countries of the world; they serve in orphanages, slum areas, homes for destitutes and the aged and so on. Baba is a strict disciplinarian and everyone associated with his service organizations perform their duties sincerely, as any lapse is bound to earn them a punishment directly or indirectly.

(3) Educational Wing: While imparting education of the highest standards in keeping with all the latest scientific know-how and technology, Baba has launched a powerful Global movement called "Education in Human Values" aimed at the moral and spiritual regeneration of mankind. The programs aim to foster a sense of Discipline, Duty, Devotion, Dedication and Determination. He says, "Work is worship. Duty is God."

As everyone is aware, India has the richest cultural and spiritual heritage in the world. Unfortunately, our education system has not paid enough attention to preserve and propagate this wonderful Vedic heritage, which is everyone's birthright, in a proper or effective manner. Here, the Bal Vikas programs seeks to remedy this flaw, by imparting the great moral, cultural and spiritual values that form part of our great heritage to children in various age-groups.

A number of schools and colleges have been opened in the Prashanti Nilayam campus, Anantapur and Brindavan campus at Whitefield. Graduate and post-graduate courses in Arts, Science and literature and Computer Sciences, are offered. A center for Computer Sciences and a Sai Space Theatre (a Planetarium) have been opened. Sri Sathya Sai Institute of higher Learning is the first university in India to have its own planetarium for educational purposes. As it is located in a rural area, it educates the rural masses about modern scientific discoveries and helps them become acquainted with basic astronomy.

A spiritual Museum at Prashanti Nilayam contains models, pictures, manuscripts, scriptures and rare quotations, teachings, films etc., of spiritual phenomena connected with all the major religions of the world. This is another example of the universal integration emphasized in Baba's teachings.

Therefore, it can be seen that the basic objectives of Baba's mission, Namasmaran (remembering or chanting the name of the Lord, according to your faith), and Seva-social service are being fully met by millions of his devotees worldwide. Baba says that every person is a divine spark born out of the Supreme Lord and is therefore basically divine in nature. Man is here on a Holy mission, a divine purpose - Man must earn his birthright, that is, Shanti (peace), which is his real nature by following the principles of Sathya (truth), Dharma (righteousness), Shanti (peace, non-violence) and Prema (love).

Baba's philosophy is that if every soul got connected with its inner, divine nature, then there would be no room for hatred or violence. To recognize that inherent quality that is at the core of every being, is the prime duty of every individual and this will be possible only when everyone turns inward, that is, Godwards.

Let us hope that with God's Grace and Baba's blessings, the object of making every single soul spiritually oriented will succeed and will usher in a world full of peace and joy and love.

SHRI KRISHNARPANAMASTU

REFERENCES

- AMMA- A BIOGRAPHY

  By Swami Amritaswarupananda Puri

- AWAKEN CHILDREN

  By Swami Amritaswarupananda Puri

- SRI SATHYA SAI BABA AND THE FUTURE OF MANKIND

  By Dr. S.P. Ruhela